Ripples in Time

Ripples in Time

Stories from a Weekend Sailor

by
Mike Mendes

SEAWORTHY PUBLICATIONS, INC. • MELBOURNE, FLORIDA

Ripples in Time
Stories from a Weekend Sailor

Paperback ISBN 978-1-966191-37-7
eBook ISBN 978-1-966191-38-4
Published in the U.S.A. by:
Seaworthy Publications, Inc.
6300 N Wickham Rd.
Unit #130-416
Melbourne, FL 32940
E-mail: orders@seaworthy.com
www.seaworthy.com

Library of Congress Cataloging-in-Publication Data
Forthcoming due to the U.S. Government shutdown.

Acknowledgments

I want to thank my wife for her support and patience. She's not a sailor but came along with me anyhow. She was always willing to pitch in and learn new things – crazy sailing terms, pulling lines and turning winch handles. Her favorite sailing activity, however, was always reading on the leeward bench.

I can't thank my Editor, Beth Hangelli, enough. She provided encouragement, wisdom, and SO much guidance and knowledge about the publishing and writing process. She read through my rough and early chapters and helped craft the final result.

Thanks also to Dakota Wolner who helped with the front cover. The cover picture is of our Santana 22 back when we were racing at Lake Dillon, and she did the blurred effect, which I think looks really cool. My foredeck guy, Craig—mentioned many times in this book—is kneeling down next to the boom.

Also, many thanks to the publisher of this book, Seaworthy Publications, Inc. As a first-time writer there wasn't much I DID know, and the team at Seaworthy very patiently and thoroughly helped me along the way, answering my dozens of dumb questions with humor.

Finally, the most thanks go to the hundreds of sailors I was lucky enough to share time with. Whether on the rail, in the cockpit, or back on shore at the bar, the times spent were some of the best of my life. Sailors are almost all generous, adventurous, and always willing to lend a hand or a tool, or advice to a fellow sailor.

Table of Contents

Acknowledgments v
Introduction viii
Foreword xv
White Squall II – A Classic Schooner 1
From the Halls of Montezuma to the Shores of Tripoli 9
God Save the Queen 15
Racing at 9,000' 28
1996 Miami Midwinters – Rubbing Elbows with Terry Hutchinson 40
Doghouse and ChuckWagon 60
The Judge 67
Psycho Duck 69
The O'Day and the Pelican (Lake, That Is) 73
Community Sailing of Colorado 81
The Blizzard Charter 90
Shenanigans 100
San Diego to Santa Barbara on Caliente 112
Fred the Boat Fix-it Guy 121
My Boat Almost Sinks 130
The Far East 26 135
America's Cup, SailGP and Rolex, Vendée Globe, and the Ultimes 140
About the Author 147

Introduction

These stories are of various sailing adventures I went on over many years, to different places and on various boats. They aren't stories of distant or exotic destinations on a beautiful cruising yacht, or of large and expensive racing machines, or of terrifying or challenging offshore passages. Rather, they are stories mostly on small boats, and lots of lakes and reservoirs.

Many thanks to the amazing people I got to share my time with on the water, and at the bar. Like many hobby enthusiasts, sailors are a pretty friendly lot and are not afraid to tip back a beer or two, sharing the day's lies and tall stories. Sailors are NOT, as many think, stuffy, rich snobs who wear blazers and white pants on their magnificent white yachts. There certainly are some of those out there, but the people I met were the antithesis of this – down to earth, humble, and ready at any time to lend a hand (or a beer) to a fellow sailor. It was not uncommon for sailors to share parts and knowledge, even with their competitors, on the racecourse the next day.

Another myth to dispel is that sailors are rich. There are many other hobbies that are vastly more expensive than sailing. And if you don't race, you can get into sailing very modestly. Racing ups the ante, depending on how serious you want to be about it. You can find small boats for a couple of thousand dollars, and if sailed off the trailer, can be very low-cost to run on a yearly basis. My current 20' boat costs about $250 for yearly insurance. My electric motor is virtually maintenance-free, but small gas outboards can be had for a few hundred dollars.

Of course, if you want to get into a proper cruising boat, you can easily spend $20,000 to $30,000 for a used 25-footer, and a lot more if you want to go coastal cruising. The J-24 is mentioned a lot in these stories, as it's a very popular boat for one-design racing and relatively easy to trailer. A good J-24 will cost $15,000, and might need new sails and gear every couple of years. It's definitely attainable for the average person.

New boats are an entirely different story. Only about 5,000 new sailboats a year are sold in the United States, which is really due to two things: new boats are incredibly expensive, and old fiberglass boats last virtually forever and are relatively easily rebuilt and refurbished. For instance, a new version of my current boat, which I paid $7,000 for, is the Corsair Pulse 600, a folding trimaran with no accommodation and only a small cubby cabin to store gear. The base price for the boat is about $39,000, which would not include trailer, engine, or a host of essential options. The out-the-door price is probably closer to $50,000. A used boat like mine makes a lot of sense.

OUR BOATS

My dad was in the oil business, and we moved around a bit. I was born in Venezuela, moved to Tripoli, Libya, when I was 4 years old, then to London, England at age 11. Many people I've met think it sounds like an awesome opportunity to live overseas, and it was. I had exposure to cultures and countries most Americans don't. But I also missed out on Friday night football, American car culture, and McDonald's. McDonald's opened a single location in London while I lived there, and we traveled over an hour by Underground to go there.

Dad's first boat was actually a little rowboat he built himself out of plywood in Oklahoma when I was about 2. It was called Lil' Jo after my Mom. It was a homely little thing with flat decks forward and aft and a very small footwell. He'd added a little outboard bracket on the aft end, but I am not sure he ever found one small enough to fit. He shipped that boat from Oklahoma all the way to Tripoli, Libya where it saw limited action before being replaced.

As long as I can remember we had sailboats, starting with a Sailfish when we moved to Tripoli, then a couple more day sailers. In England, we had four cruisers: 27' Albin Vega, 30' Albin Ballad, 29' Westerly Konsort, and a Sadler 34. When my parents moved to Colorado, my dad's interest in boats did not stop: the boats just got smaller and trailerable. His first Colorado boat was an Ericson 25, a proper little cruiser in the vein of the boats he used to own in England. But it was very heavy and not suitable for Lake Dillon, which is where he kept his first boats. That was followed by a Santana 22, then a Precision 21, a Cal 20, a Precision 23 (or P23), then another Precision, this time the 18, then a Com-Pac Sun Cat and finally another Precision 21, which he owned until he couldn't sail any longer. There were 15 in all, and every one was named Flood Tide, which was a name taken from an old family member who'd had a couple of large sailing yachts named Flood Tide.

Dad was a tinkerer, and never had a boat that didn't need some of the "Bob Mendes" touch. There are lots of funny sayings about boats and the costs of ownership: "Boats are holes in the water into which we pour money," "Cruising is fixing boats in exotic places," and "BOAT stands for Bust Out Another Thousand." Dad preferred to do a lot of the work himself, and he was pretty creative and good at it. When we had our boats in England, battery-powered tools had not yet been invented, so he did everything with hand tools. He drilled, sawed, and sanded everything the old-fashioned way. Only when we were "on the hard" (i.e., on stands in the boat yard at the end of the season) could he run an extension cord and use power tools.

Most small cruising boats came with large cockpit lockers that had no shelves or any way to keep the contents organized. So, he built many plywood and fiberglass shelves. In the Colorado boats, he decided the designers had not planned in enough ballast, so he added lead plugs on top of the lead keel. I always wondered if this actually had any real effect, but he swore by it, and every single Precision got this treatment.

My mom thought I had learned my own boat repair skills from Dad, but this was not the case. He rarely had me help him, and I wasn't too interested as a teenager in any case. I learned my own repair skills by trial and error, and everyone's "go to" source – Google.

I will cover the cruising boats we owned in England in some detail, but the trailerables became a bit of an obsession. He'd no sooner get one "just the way he liked it," then he would move on to another boat, with little logical reasoning to justify the decision. The Santana 22 was our first race boat, and I ended up buying him out of that one since he was not that interested in racing. The Precisions were very nice little boats, quite well built and practical for their size. He almost always sailed single-handed, so ease of handling was important.

The boat he should never have sold was the Sun Cat, made by Com-Pac. We had occasion to tour some sailboat factories on the west coast of Florida as a father/son activity, and we had the Com-Pac factory on our list. They had a couple of small cruisers, relatively heavy displacement and quality built, in the 16' to 23' range. As Dad got older, the need for ease of handling became more and more critical. We had gone through the factory and had seen a smaller boat called a Sun Cat. It was only 17', but had a huge cockpit, a small cabin, and was very beamy. Most importantly, it had a single cat-rigged sail (no jib), hence the name Sun Cat. This ensured easy handling.

I spied this boat and thought it looked like a good option for an older sailor. As we were leaving the factory, after seeing several other Com-Pac boats, I suggested he take a closer look, so we turned around and went back in. A few months later, he had an order in for a brand-new one, with a beautiful navy blue hull and cream-colored topsides and cockpit. She was cute as a button, and he enjoyed that boat for several seasons. But he got the buy bug again, and sold her to be replaced by another Precision, which was much less suitable for a now 70-year-old. This became apparent one day on Aurora Reservoir, where he kept his boats in the last years.

* * *

Aurora Reservoir is a nice enough spot. It was pretty far east of Denver, owned and managed by the City of Aurora, and they allowed only about 20 boats on moorings. (A mooring is usually a block of concrete on the lake bottom with a length of chain and a float attached to it, to which you attach your boat.) There was no marina or slips, nor was anyone allowed to anchor on their own, or swim off their boats. They did not allow gas motors of any kind (except those used by their own Park Rangers), so there were no jet skis, wake boats, or water skiers. Fishing was allowed as long as you used an electric motor. This meant that only sailboats were allowed on the moorings, and they had to be electric driven.

Getting to your boat was a bit of a process. There was an aluminum courtesy fishing boat (A "tinny," as the Aussies call them.) you used to row to your mooring. Then, on your way out for your sail, you would drop it back at the dock until you returned. For a little while, Dad brought his own little inflatable boat in his SUV and used that to row out. However, it was very difficult to row, didn't take more than one person, and had little carrying capacity for gear, coolers, and the like. The reward for all the effort was a body of water that was almost always empty of any other craft, except fishermen. It also generally had better wind than reservoirs closer to the mountains.

Dad's boats were always relatively light and small, and so an electric trolling motor was a good fit. He really only needed to get out of the little mooring area and into the main lake basin, which was a couple hundred yards. The electric motor couldn't push the boat against a strong wind, so Dad kept a good eye on the horizon. Being closer to the plains, there was a greater chance for summer afternoon thunderstorms.

One day, I arranged to meet him at the boat. When I arrived, I found him out on the lake in a good 20 knots of wind, completely out of control. Apparently, the battery for the electric motor was dead and he was trying to sail back to the mooring into the wind with just the main, which for some reason was about a third of the way down. This meant he had little control and was bashing back and forth, making no progress toward his mooring. It was clear he had panicked and was not thinking things through, which was odd for him. But he was about 75 now, and his thought processes were not as sharp as they once were.

I jumped in the courtesy boat and rowed out to him. He was quite frazzled and definitely not thinking clearly. When the motor had not started for the trip home, he got confused and started making wrong decisions. The first thing was to get the main all the way down, as it had jammed in the track with the pressure from the wind. He had forgotten there was a second battery on board: he had one for the electric motor and another to run the lights on the boat. So, I pulled that out, connected it, and we were back up and running. It was an easy return trip to the mooring, where we could sort everything out.

It was one of the last times he went sailing, as the event scared both him and Mom. He realized he was not as capable as he used to be, physically or mentally. I am pretty sure if he'd kept the Sun Cat, he would have more easily been able to think through his options more logically and douse the main and get the boat under control. It is amazing how once things start going sideways on a sailboat, they can just snowball. It was an inauspicious end to a lifetime of sailing.

We sold that last Precision to a very nice doctor a short time later, and Dad's long love affair with sailing and boats came to an end. But there was one more story to tell. Like all of Dad's boats, he kept the P21 in excellent condition, and it sold quickly. We met the new owner out at the reservoir, signed the papers, and agreed to tow the boat to the buyer's house. I was to follow the boat and trailer, with Dad and the buyer in the tow vehicle, in my own car. On the way out on the main road to E-470, the right rear wheel on the trailer started to wobble. Then, I saw something that looked like shrapnel blow out the side of the wheel. This, of course, was the bearings. I called Dad on his cell and told him to pull over, since they hadn't noticed anything.

It turns out that if you need to find roadside service for a boat trailer, 18-wheeler service guys are the ones to call. Our tech came out quickly enough and said he needed a day and some parts, but could do the work right there the next day – for $900! (It needed a new axle.) The purchase price for the boat was $8,500, so this was a substantial sum. Technically, the boat was already the buyer's, since the paperwork had been signed and funds changed hands. But we were not going to stick this bill on the buyer and felt terrible that this happened literally a few minutes into his new ownership, so offered to cover the cost. The doctor was a real gentleman and agreed to split it with us.

The next day, the repair was completed and the good doctor had his boat. I saw it at Cherry Creek Reservoir for several seasons, and it gave me satisfaction to see Flood Tide in the water.

MOTIVATION AND MAGIC

Many people are lured to sailing by the romance of it. Some have dreams of sailing the world and visiting far-off countries in their own vessel. One of my favorite YouTube channels, Nick and Teryse of Sailing Ruby Rose, recently shared their motivation for buying a blue water cruiser. They are a delightful couple who have sailed and cruised much of the world, first on a 38' monohull and now a Seawind 1370 catamaran. When Nick was young, his parents vacationed in Greece, specifically in Rhodes. He spent time down at the harbor dock, dreaming of the day he could return to Rhodes in his own boat. In December of 2024, he was able to attain that goal.

Some people are pure racers – and I can attest to the obsessive nature of racing. It really gets in your blood. Not only are you competing against the other boats and sailors, but the wind, weather, and water as well. It's a high-level chess game, and many millionaires and billionaires spend large fortunes racing their boats.

For me, it's pretty simple: I just love being in a boat driven by the wind. It's kind of what we all want – something for nothing. The wind is free, and we go sailing and are able to be moved by it. The way the boat moves through the water like a living thing brings me peace like nothing else. And I don't need a big boat or anything fancy to achieve the peace that sailing gives me. It must go back to my childhood, when I would go out with my dad as young as 4 years of age. Our little Sailfish felt like a spaceship cutting through the warm waters of the Mediterranean. I never get tired of it. And I suppose it's some of the reason I resent the jet skis and wave boats: they ruin my tranquility and connection with nature. I also don't care too much if the weather isn't perfect. Regardless of the conditions, sailing is better than just about anything I can think of.

Foreword

There are tons of books about people who sold everything and went cruising, experiencing harrowing weather and adventures along the way – Joshua Slocum, Sir Francis Chichester, and Sir Robin Knox Johnston.

There are lots of great books about and by skilled racers – Dennis Conner, Peter Isler, Larry Ellison, and Peter Blake. Also, amazing stories of the brave men who went to sea without the modern aids we have today, to find new lands or riches for king or queen and country – Magellan, Darwin, Cook, Columbus.

The reality is that a very small percentage of sailors have the imagination, motivation, or money to abandon their land lives and sail off into the sunset. There are far more sailors like me – weekend warriors, beer can racers, small lake and reservoir sailors, and coastal cruisers – who just love to sail. Some of us have grander boats and bank accounts than others, but we are either not interested or do not have the resources to go blue water cruising. We're just happy to get away from daily life for a while and be at peace on the water.

I hope my stories will be enjoyable to "regular" sailors and rock stars alike, and remind you of your good and bad days spent on the water.

So, pour yourself a dram and let's go sailing!

Many thanks to the hundreds of sailors I've met over 60+ years who inspired me to write this book, especially Brandon and Melissa who got me back into sailing after a long layoff. Also, to my editor, Beth, who doesn't even like sailing! Her knowledge of the publishing industry and her patience with me helped immensely. I could not have done it without her. And of course, I have to thank my wife Kathy for her support and unconditional love, even though her idea of sailing is laying on the cockpit bench reading.

Chapter One

White Squall II – A Classic Schooner

When I was 6 years old, my dad chartered a 67' schooner called White Squall II. (Nothing to do with the movie.) It was owned and run by Ross Norgrove, who had sailed her from New Zealand across the Pacific to start his charter business in the British Virgin Islands. His first mate and cook was also his wife. This was 1964, and the BVI were almost completely devoid of pleasure yachts. The bareboat charter craze was still a few years away, and we mostly had every anchorage completely to ourselves. There were some day trip boats out of Tortola that brought tourists to places like The Baths, but many of the now-overrun stopping places, like Peter Island, Virgin Gorda, or Jost Van Dyke, were deserted.

The trip was substantial, as we lived in Tripoli, Libya, far from major flight hubs. We took a flight to Rome, then New York, then San Juan, then Tortola in the BVI. It took over a day each way.

Ross was a brilliant seaman and entertaining skipper. Evenings were enjoyed with some guitar or ukulele songs. The yacht was schooner rigged with a large main mast and smaller forward mast. There were two jibs and a fifth sail called a Fisherman, could be flown between the two masts. Everything was made of wood. While there was a rudimentary winch with a huge brass handle, much of the sail control was done with strong backs and legs. Guests were encouraged (required?) to help.

For a 67-footer, the interior accommodations were cramped. The hull was designed and built in the '30s, and so had a very narrow beam and huge, deep keel. There were long overhangs and a huge bowsprit. She was 60 tons, which by today's standards is grossly obese.

All woodwork was dark mahogany, which didn't help with the sense of feeling small inside. There were three cabins, plus the salon. Ross and his wife Marion occupied the V-berth forward. The main guest cabin was aft of that, then the galley. The main salon was large, with a huge, gimbaled table and an overhead "butterfly" skylight.

The main engine room was aft of that, then the second guest cabin, which is where my sister and I ended up. Air flow in this cabin was not great and there was a lot of smell from the engine, so it was not the first choice for guests, even though it was larger than the forward cabin. At every stop, a large canopy was tied up over the main salon and our cabin. My sister and I frequently chose to sleep on deck, where there were a couple of sun pads. At 6 years old, I wasn't too fussy about the quality of the mattress!

All of the things that make the BVI such a great cruising ground today were true back then, plus some. The water was crystal clear. You could see details in the sandy bottom at 60'. Coral reefs were vibrant and colorful, and teeming with fish. At one stop, I saw a nurse shark on the sea bottom and asked Ross if it was real, as if Ross had placed it there for my amusement. This was a joke told by my dad for decades.

The breeze was constant, 12 to 18 knot westerlies. This was good news for such a heavy boat with lots of surface area. White Squall II with all sail up in 18 knots of wind was truly a magnificent sight. There were no electronics, so I have no idea how fast we were going, but I am sure she was capable of 10 to 12 knots on a reach in these conditions. And unlike the lightweight designs of today, she would shrug off all but the biggest of waves in the mostly protected waters of the Sir Francis Drake Channel.

If you've never chartered a yacht, life gets into a certain kind of blissful rhythm. Wake up when you want, usually with the sun. Enjoy a leisurely breakfast, then decide what to do for the day. A short sail in warm breezes and sparkling sun to a snorkeling destination. Gaze at amazing fish and sea life before lunch, followed by another sail for the night stop. Then, play with water toys, or more snorkeling.

In the '60s, water toys had not really been invented, so no SUPs, kayaks, or water skiing. Ross rigged a "Geronimo line," a long halyard that could be swung across the flat deck forward of the main mast. Hanging on allowed you to swing way out over the water before falling 10' or more to the water. We spent many hours doing this, as it was endless fun. The adults would enjoy a beverage and quiet time as the sun set, followed by dinner, songs, and early to bed. All to be repeated the next day.

One great advantage of a crewed charter (versus a bareboat charter, when the boat is run by the charterers) is that the meals and yacht operation were handled by the crew. Most crewed yachts have good cooks or chefs on board and the bigger the yacht, the better they were likely to be (and the better the ingredients used). Also, the higher the charter price. Food becomes an important part of the day, and not having to worry about preparing meals makes the whole experience that much better.

* * *

We were lucky enough to charter White Squall II for a second time two years later, when I was 8. Marion was gone, replaced by Davey, a mid-20s "free spirit" who was not as good a cook, but an enjoyable crew nonetheless. Dad took lots of 8mm movies without sound, which he spliced together into a 20-minute movie of our charters. We loved showing this to anyone who had ever chartered or worked in the BVI, as the complete lack of any other yachts of any kind is in very stark contrast to the hordes of people and boats that flock there every year now.

Ross died in the mid '80s of cancer, which was a cruel fate for such a vibrant and outgoing man. I saw White Squall II decades later, doing day charters out of Tortola. She was then abandoned and left to rot in a backwater, until some Polish sailors decided to try to bring her back to life. They did enough work to make her seaworthy and sailed her back to Poland, where she was to be refit. There's a Facebook page about the yacht, but it stops in 2017, so I suspect they ran out of money and/or enthusiasm. A wooden hull left to rot would be a huge project to bring back to life. As of this writing, I don't know where she is. Like her old owner, it would be a sad ending for a grand old lady.

* * *

We were lucky enough to charter in the BVI three more times, all crewed. The first was on Prelude, a stunning North Wind 56' sailing sloop. While she was fully 11' shorter than White Squall II, her interior accommodations were significantly larger. She had a huge full beam master cabin aft with a queen-sized walk around berth, two more midships double cabins, and a large forepeak cabin for the crew. There was also a huge main saloon and a massive galley.

Our crew were Kathy and John, perfect hosts for a week cruising the BVI. She was a tall, slim, and pretty American; he was English, with an appropriate dry sense of humor. They had some pretty good banter, and she was an amazing cook. My daughter at the time was about 4 years old and learning to read, so Kathy spent many hours reading with her. It was adorable. It was probably the best crewed charter we ever had. We found out later that they had split up: she had gone back to San Francisco and wanted to have kids, he did not. So, he moved on to other charter yachts.

Our next charter was on Promenade, a 65' trimaran that is still working in the BVI as a charter boat. This time, my sister and her family came along (except her husband, who didn't do boats), so ten of us in all. We had five crew in total this time, with the skipper being a woman and her First Mate of uncertain relationship. There were also two young female stewardesses and a deckhand/dive guy. My (then) wife and I were certified divers, so were looking forward to diving with him. We did a wreck and a night dive, both of which were amazing. They had a 22' tender with a 70 HP engine, so could speed all over the place. We needed to get 20 miles to the wreck. No problem, 30 minutes in the tender!

The whole feel of this charter was completely different. With 15 people on board, it might sound like it should have been cramped, but the boat was huge. One would expect it to be a good sailing boat, being a Nigel Irens design, but it was so overladen with people and stuff that it was not. We mostly motored everywhere. It needed at least 15 knots to get going, and didn't go to weather at all. It was about the only disappointing thing about this charter compared to Promenade, which was a great sailing boat. My sister has three kids and I have two, and they were all within about five years of each other. So, lots of water fun was had by all. This time, there were kayaks, and some of us also tried knee boarding behind the large powerboat.

It is hard to explain the magic of the BVI. And why not the USVI? The U.S. side of the archipelago is far more built up, there aren't as many good cruising spots to swim and snorkel, and generally it's just not as desirable as the BVI side. The BVI surround the Sir Francis Drake Channel, which provides a bit of protection from the almost-constant westerly trade winds. The wave action is a bit tamped down here, and there are many great anchorages a few hours' sail on both sides of the Channel.

Road Town on the island of Tortola is the center of the charter companies. When we went in the late '60s, it was barely a village, with a small-town center and brightly painted cottages clinging to the hillsides to the north. The main airport is on Beef Island, at the far east end of Tortola. A hair-raising cab ride into Road Town was always guaranteed, as cars, trucks, pedestrians, cattle and other animals, bikes and children competed for the narrow strip of asphalt they called a road.

One of the charms of the BVI are the names of their islands and attractions. The world-famous Willy T's is on Norman Island. The Indians, a couple of rocks off the northern tip of Norman, are a favorite daytime snorkeling spot. Then, there's Salt Island, Virgin Gorda with the Bitter End Yacht Club, the Dog Islands, Jost Van Dyke (with the Soggy Dollar Bar), and The Baths.

The Baths is a rock formation of giant boulders that have been worn smooth over millennia. There are little pools in and amongst the rocks to explore. When we first came here, you could bring your dinghy right on shore. Now, you have to tie up offshore a couple hundred yards and swim in. They have also built stairs and provided ropes to help people get around more easily, which kind of ruins the rugged effect of the place. Exploring and making your own way was one of the attractions of The Baths. The water is always warm and clear, and the increase in charter boats has not diminished this in any way.

Road Town is now a bustling small city, with all the pros and cons that go with it. Do you need several large grocery stores to provision from? No problem. Good restaurants and nightlife? Check. There are literally hundreds of charter boats here now, available from several different companies.

The last charter was just my family and my parents again, this time on a Beneteau 50. It was a fine boat and had a good crew. I don't remember much of it, except one spectacular sail to Anegada, an island off the beaten track – one that we had never been to in all our BVI trips. It's a 15-mile sail from the north of Virgin Gorda, so a several-hour sail in more open water than much of the BVI. The island itself is very flat, with a maximum elevation of 28' and a population of 450. Miles of creamy white beaches are on the north side, so a quick taxi ride is strongly suggested. There was nothing north of the island but the North Atlantic for hundreds of miles, so you really did feel like you were on the edge of the earth. Our return trip home was in 20 knots on a beam reach and the Beneteau was hitting 10 to 11 knots, even with a lot of people and gear on board.

Dad paid for all of these charters and many other family vacations, as his investment accounts did well. As long as the stock market was going up, we'd have a grand yearly family vacation. Sailboat charters were his favorite, but they excluded my sister's husband, as he didn't do boats. So, Dad included other amazing destinations, like Hawaii, Disney, Captiva Island in Florida, and the Cayman Islands, which we visited three times.

* * *

Our first time in the Cayman Islands, we had two condos on the popular Seven Mile Beach. My sister and I were tasked with buying groceries and arranging meals – not a trivial thing for 11 people! Seven Mile Beach was not really our scene, as it was very built up and the road to Georgetown was always busy. There was OK snorkeling in the bay right outside the condos, but not as good as the BVI. So, the next two visits, Dad rented a house on a beach on the other side of the island, called Sand Point. It was a 30- to 40-minute drive from George Town, but worth it to have privacy and direct water access to the North Sound on our own beach and swimming pool.

It is hard to explain the spectacular water in this area. Unlike the BVI, where the water is mostly deeper and so has a dark blue color, the water off our beach was quite shallow and over very bright, white sand. This gave the water an amazing turquoise color and ensured it was always warm.

The North Sound was also the home of Stingray City, surely one of the most astonishing natural phenomena on earth. The North Sound has a line of reefs protecting the water behind them, where the water is as shallow as 3 feet. It is believed that fisherman cleaned their day's catch here, providing an easy meal for stingrays. Over the years, they have stayed to be fed daily by tourists taken there in large groups.

Dad rented a smaller power boat and a personal guide to take us out. The rays collect in large numbers, many dozens at a time. We all jumped in and were delighted to be in the water with these amazing creatures (except my mom, who was a scaredy-cat). They swam right up to us and rubbed their undersides against our legs and hands. While the tops of their bodies are quite rough and leathery, their undersides are as soft as a baby's bottom. Feeding needed to be done carefully, as a hand and food could be easily confused. You also had to be very careful where you stepped so as to not accidentally step on one of them covered in sand on the bottom. A cut or stab from a stingray's tail can be painful, but almost never fatal. Like many natural areas, the mobs of people have spoiled it a bit, but it was still worth the trip.

The second villa we rented was after Hurricane Ivan damaged much of the island. We had a beautiful private beach, with a large swimming pool and a private boat dock. Tangled in the bushes by the water was a Sunfish, very tattered and beat up by the hurricane. I pulled it out and took a look, and it was not as bad as it first looked – a testament to fiberglass construction! The sail was still intact, as was most of the hardware. The fitting that held the lateen rigged sail to the mast was gone, but the boat had been wrapped up in a pile of yellow polypropylene rope. Not having any tools did not deter me, and I did my best MacGyver job on the little boat. I lashed the gaff to the mast and fashioned a mainsheet, all from the crappy yellow poly rope.

This rental villa was on the protected side of the peninsula, and we had a beautiful little bay ½ mile by 2 miles all to ourselves. My dad and I spent many hours in that Sunfish, sailing back and forth in the warm, crystal-clear blue-green waters. The trade winds were warm and consistent, and we blasted around without a care in the world. Like so many of my sailing experiences, the simplest were often the most enjoyable. I felt a pang of sadness leaving that little survivor of a boat. I hope that someone did a proper job of bringing her back to life.

Chapter Two

From the Halls of Montezuma to the Shores of Tripoli

I was born in Venezuela, in a little camp near the oil company town of San Tome. My dad was born in Tobago and his father in Trinidad. My family originally was Portuguese, having first immigrated to the island of Madeira due to religious persecution. They were Protestants in a country of Catholics. They moved to Trinidad around 1900. My grandfather ran a coconut plantation and guest house called Bacolet until a hurricane wiped him out. But for that storm, I could very well be a coconut plantation owner today.

My father went to boarding school in upstate New York, then to the University of Oklahoma for a Petroleum Geologist degree, where he met my mother. He got a job with Texaco that would take him to Venezuela. He asked my mom and sister to join him, and I was born shortly afterwards. Following the stint in Venezuela, there was a short stop in Oklahoma, then he took a job in Tripoli, Libya, where vast reserves of oil had been discovered.

The name Mendes is Portuguese in origin, so there are many Mendes in Portugal and Brazil, where they also speak Portuguese. If it sounds familiar, there are a couple of famous namesakes. Eva Mendes is a well-known actress. There is an Eva in our family tree but alas, they are not the same. Younger readers know of Shaun Mendes, a well-known pop star.

Our most famous namesake is Sam, my third cousin. He is my grandfather's brother's grandson. I am not sure if a third cousin is even a thing. He has had quite an amazing career on both screen and stage, having been nominated for four Academy Awards, winning for American Beauty. (He should have also won for 1917, which is one of the best war movies ever made.) He also won four BAFTAs and three Golden Globes, as well as two Tony Awards and three Olivier Awards (London's West End equivalent of the Tony Award). He also directed the widely acclaimed James Bond movie Skyfall. It is entirely possible Sam does not know I exist, as we have never met. His father Peter and my dad met in London once, but there was no other communication between the families, as far as I know. Shame.

Tripoli is on the Mediterranean Sea. There are lines of reefs offshore that provide a very nice, protected area close to shore. The water is clear and the beaches beautiful. Libya had a mandatory half-day religious holiday every Friday, so our weekends were two and a half days long! We spent a LOT of time sailing and at the beach. It was warm to hot nine months of the year. In fact, while we lived there, the highest temperature ever recorded worldwide was just outside the city: 136°! This was before Qaddafi took over, and the political scene was pretty calm. When he took power in 1969, he deported all non-Libyans, so we had to leave (by USAF freight transport). I was 11 years old.

Beach and sailing time are seen through a rose-colored perspective when you're that age, and I was no exception. The time we spent down at the water was amazing. At that age, you don't notice the heat as much, and the water was always a welcome relief.

Our first sailboat was a Sailfish, a predecessor to the Sunfish, very similar in design and size. There was barely enough room for two, so I got to go more than Mom or my sister as I was the smallest. Dad gave me the helm when I was around 6 years old, with some gentle coaching. The boat was lively and quite fast on a reach or downwind – and also wet. That didn't matter much, as we were always in swimsuits and the water was warm.

Our second boat was a Flying Junior, a very nice 14' open dinghy, with a lot more room for all of us. It had comfy seats and a better all-around sail plan. There was no racing, and my dad wasn't really interested in racing anyhow. But we could bring along a cooler and there was a small anchor, so we could pull up next to the many reefs and enjoy the fish and excellent coral. Tripoli was a huge exporter of oil (both then and now), but the coastline was essentially undeveloped, as was most of the rest of the country. There were very few other boats. The locals had fishing boats, but there were only a handful of recreational boats. This meant that everywhere we went we had to ourselves.

Boat #3 in Tripoli was a Maraudeur, a French-built cuddy cabin boat that gave us a chance to start "cruising." To say that this was barely more than camping on the water would be an understatement. There was no head or sink, just a couple of small V berths with crappy cushions. I am pretty sure we didn't even have a battery or nav lights – a bit risky at night! I got to sleep in the cockpit, which at about 8 years old was not a huge issue. My mom would bring cold baked chicken from home with homemade potato salad. Water was from a jug, and you better not have to go number 2 or you'd be in trouble. Chicken bones were fed to the fish, much to my delight.

* * *

Tripoli at this time was ruled by King Idris, and Libya was mostly made up of Bedouins, nomadic Arabs who somehow managed to survive in the brutal conditions of the Sahara Desert. With an area about 10% larger than Alaska, the sparse population of about 3 million at the time had lots of room. There was a small strip along the coast where some hot-weather crops could survive (mostly fruit trees and olives). Tripoli was by far the largest city. Bedouins who tried to find work around the city would set up "shanty towns" of corrugated metal and plywood. These encampments made a big impression on me as a boy. Little Arab boys would take the wheel from a busted bike, remove the spokes, and push it around with a stick. Or play soccer with a wadded-up ball of rags. It seemed like a million miles away from the transported American suburbia we lived in.

Our home was made of sandstone and concrete, with tile floors and walls over a foot thick. This helped with the blistering heat of the day and made home improvements very interesting for my dad. We finally added a wall-mounted air conditioner that he had to cut a huge hole in the wall to accommodate. The house was surrounded by a concrete wall 6' tall. Our "street" was sand that would wash out when it rained hard, creating some fun for little kids.

Bugs were everywhere and grew to an impressive size. Beetles were 2" to 3" long, and we had REAL cockroaches of the same dimensions. We had a big caster bean tree in the back yard that the cockroaches decided to use as a hotel. One evening, my dad filled an old metal spray gun and pumped the tree full of gasoline. The roaches poured out, like something out of a Hitchcock movie! We also frequently found scorpions and great big bumblebees.

Living in Tripoli as a boy was mostly a lot of fun, as I got to climb trees and play in the sand. Most of the Americans there worked for oil companies, so they built a school for the kids called the Oil Companies School, or OCS. This was a few miles from our house. We had bus service, or we could ride our bikes when we got older. The school was for grades K through 8 and had about 1,500 students. There were sand ballfields, a gym, and a large number of classroom buildings made of concrete. There was no A/C, so the searing daytime heat could be a real problem. Falling asleep in the heat was not hard. After 8th grade, you either went to high school on the local Air Force Base, Wheelus, or to boarding school in Europe, which is what my sister did.

Dad bought the Sailfish without a trailer, so he built one out of 2x4s and a couple of bicycle wheels. We towed this with the preferred vehicle of choice in Tripoli – the VW Beetle. We ended up owning two of these cute little cars. They were good on the sandy roads that were everywhere, except the very largest highways. The local kids used to pile up sand at well-traveled corners, where you had to slow and would likely get stuck. They would then push you out for some "baksheesh" or payment. And if you didn't pay, you would sit there, in the way. With no cell phones, you were very much at their mercy. It was a real scam, but kind of funny in hindsight.

The boat was parked in the back yard, and my friend from down the street and I discovered it made a pretty good teeter-totter. Problem was, it was not designed to take the loads two 6-year-olds could put on it rocking back and forth, and we cracked one of the main beams.

Dad discovered this when he got home and spanked me as hard as I ever had been. I had never seen him so angry. Needless to say, I used better judgment in the future.

We played Little League baseball and just like home, the competition between teams and yelling dads was intense (and ridiculous). I was not very good, although I did hit two home runs. It put me off baseball for the rest of my life. It was a terribly boring game for anyone but the pitcher and catcher and in the overbearing heat, standing around was not fun.

Tripoli was on the edge of the Sahara Desert. Living there, we were subject to something called a Ghibli. This is a storm that comes from the south across the vast expanse of the desert, over 1,000 miles. When the winds were strong, huge amounts of sand would pile up in drifts in our yards and streets, just like snow. But unlike snow, it didn't melt, but required removal by earth diggers and shovels. It was sometimes impossible to be outside when the storms were particularly bad. Not only was visibility dangerously low, but sand would get in every crack and crevice of your body, including your eyes. Even with storm shutters, sand would get in the house, providing a constant battle for my mom to keep things clean.

We would also occasionally get storms from the north that came across the Mediterranean Sea. Directly north of Tripoli is the island of Sicily, some 300 miles away. These storms were a lot nicer than the Ghiblis, as they would be cool and humid, a rare occurrence in our part of the world.

* * *

In 1969, I was waiting for the school bus at the end of my street, which was on the edge of the major highway that runs along the coast. The bus never showed; however, a long column of tanks and troop carriers started driving down the road, away from the city center. It turned out that Qaddafi had overthrown King Idris and his government in a coup. Idris had been out of the country and Qaddafi, at the time only a Colonel in the army, managed to convince the army to join him.

Idris only had a small number of police to defend his throne, and the coup was bloodless.

While Idris had kept much of the oil wealth for himself and his family, Qaddafi created schools, a health care system, and a form of representative government. He generally funneled much of the country's wealth back to the people. We in the West thought he was a nut, as his public persona of being a tough guy and thumbing his nose at the U.S., UK, and Europe seemed silly and childish. But he actually did a lot of good for the people of the country.

I went back home and Dad came home midday, which never happened. Qaddafi had ordered all foreigners to leave the country immediately, so Dad told us to pack a single bag each. We drove out to Wheelus Air Force Base and were loaded onto a C130 for transport to Naples, Italy, then back to the US. This was close to the end of the school year, so we spent the summer with my grandmother in Muskegon, Michigan. In a couple of weeks, Dad was allowed to go back to Tripoli to pack up the house.

Qaddafi, being the sly fox he was, nationalized the oil companies, but left them with a 49% stake, so they would be incentivized to leave staff and resources in the country. Libya, of course, had little infrastructure of its own, so this was a wise move. A junior geologist in Dad's office was Libyan. He'd gone to school in the U.S. and was one of the few Libyans who had any training in the oil business. At 28, Qaddafi made him his oil minister! My dad was called to meet with this young man a few weeks later, and who was also in the room but Qaddafi himself! He didn't say anything, but my dad was definitely unnerved.

Qaddafi met a grisly end in 2011, when his government was itself overthrown in a very bloody coup.

When we left for the Air Force base earlier in the summer, we didn't know that we would never see our Tripoli home again, or enjoy the stunning clear waters of the Mediterranean. Dad took a job in London, England, so after our summer vacation, we headed there.

Chapter Three
God Save the Queen

When we moved from Tripoli to London in 1969, I was 11 years old. I entered sixth grade in mid-September, so I was a bit behind. The U.K.'s education system is designed differently than the U.S.'s, so there were a couple of American schools in London. Mine was the American School in London (ASL). At that time, it occupied several row houses on the south side of Regent's Park. A new school building that would house all grades and approximately 1,500 students was being built that would open for middle school students the next year. But for the time being, we were spread out across three separate facilities around the Park. There was no gym and barely a cafeteria, so we took physical education classes in the Park. It was a weird and awkward transition for me, coming from hot and dry Libya to cold and rainy London.

We found a flat about 2 miles north of the new school building. It had three bedrooms, two bathrooms, and was only 1,100 square feet. We were on the first floor (the second floor in the U.S.) of a seven-story building. My standard-sized bed barely fit width-wise in my bedroom. There was space for a desk and a small closet, and that was it. Open space outdoors was at a premium in a densely populated city of eight million, and there weren't many places to play for a high-energy kid. Primrose Hill was a couple of miles away, the result of thousands of tons of rubble from the WW II bombing being piled up in one place. At 210' in elevation, it was a sobering reminder of dark times. We ran here for basketball practice, and I used it for sledding on the very rare occasions that we had snow. It was also a great place to look at the city of London.

We played in the hallways and the back alley of our building, which got us into trouble. There was another kid on my floor about my age who lived at the end of the hallway. There were only four apartments per floor. We played soccer with a beach ball in the hallway, with our respective doorways as goals. That was, until one of the neighbors would come out and shoo us off. Or call the building superintendent, who would come up blazing mad and yell at us. So, we would take to the alley behind the building, where the garages for the owners were. This would also get the attention of the powers that be, and we'd once again have to bail.

The Brits definitely believed in the saying, "Children should be seen and not heard"!

One great thing about growing up in London was having access to public transportation, which was excellent. Besides the Underground (called the Tube), the bus system was convenient and usually on time. Since ASL didn't have buses to collect kids, I had to take a public bus 10 miles or so to get to school, before we moved into our flat. Once the new school opened, it was about a 15-minute walk. But I could get anywhere in the city on buses and the Tube. It was great.

The concert scene in London was amazing, as any big act coming to Europe stopped there at some point. Tickets were cheap, and being able to take public transport eliminated the need (or worry) of driving anywhere. I saw America, John Denver, ELO, Chuck Berry, Genesis, Grand Funk Railroad, the Steve Miller Band, and Deep Purple, among others, for between $3 and $10.

In 1972, I was a freshman in high school. Somehow, our Student Council talked Elton John into playing in our gym. We could pack about 1,500 people onto the old-school bleachers and folding chairs. It was an incredible event for a high school! Some of the high school students helped set up the stage and sound system. The next year, he came back with Kiki Dee. Unfortunately, someone found a copy of the simply printed tickets and made a bunch of illegal copies. So, the venue was way oversold, with people packed into every corner. Still, it was an incredible concert, just as Elton was becoming an international superstar.

* * *

My dad brought the 16' Maraudeur to England with us, and it was clear from the first sail that she was completely the wrong tool for the job. We kept our boats at Swanwick Marina, also called Moody's, named after the owners who went on to become yacht builders of some fame. This was quite far up the Hamble River and gave us access to the Solent, a strip of water between the south coast of England and the Isle of Wight. The IOW was a diamond-shaped island, with the port of Cowes at its northern tip. The Solent was a fairly narrow strip of water, ranging from a couple of miles to perhaps six or seven miles wide. Tides were brisk, running at 2 to 3 knots through the main channel. Winds likewise could be strong, frequently blowing 20+ knots and up on bad days. The Solent emptied out to the English Channel on both ends.

Getting to the marina was quite a trip. It required a taxi or Tube ride to Waterloo Station, which was on the south side of the Thames River. We lived pretty far north of the main city center, in St. John's Wood. Then, we took a train to Southampton, then another train to Bursledon. Once we were there, it was a half-mile walk to the marina. This was a solid three-hour journey in total, and the last half mile could be a killer when hauling a pile of boat parts, clothes, gear, etc. As Dad got older, he was more inclined to take taxis to and from Waterloo, which suited Mom and me just fine. Rarely would he hire a car for the whole trip, unless we were opening the boat for the season and had a lot of gear to take down.

Our first sail in the Maraudeur was not in bad weather or unusually large waves, but the little boat was clearly uncomfortable in the chop. And it was a wet ride, as we were quite low in the water: even small waves came over the bow and into the cockpit. It was obvious we needed something a lot bigger, especially as we were hoping to cruise the many little harbors and anchorages that dotted both the IOW and southern England on both sides of the Solent. The search was on right away for a more suitable replacement.

We looked at a number of boats between about 22' and 28'. I was 11 years old at the time and all of them looked huge, compared to our little cuddy cabin boat and the dinghies before that. We settled on an Albin Vega, a 27-footer built in Sweden. It was a huge sales success all over the world, selling over 3,500 boats during its production run.

The boat had a main cabin, small enclosed (well, sort of enclosed) head, and a fore cabin with a V-berth. There was standing headroom in the main cabin for us shorter men and plenty for my mom, who was only 5' 1." There was lots of teak, but not particularly well finished, a small galley on either side of the main companionway, and long single berths on either side of the main cabin. There was good storage behind the removable back rests, and many other nooks and crannies for storage. There was an old-school hand-pump toilet in a small area and a clever pull-out sink that drained into the toilet, but no shower. There was a folding door to the main cabin and a curtain to the V-berth. Mom and Dad slept in the main cabin and I had the forepeak. This suited me just fine, as I had a little privacy.

The Vega had a relatively shallow, long keel – not quite a traditional full-length keel, but also not a more modern (for the time) fin keel. There wasn't quite enough ballast in this keel, and we found the boat to be quite tender, which meant it wanted to round up into the wind when the wind speed was 13 to 14 knots (which was often). We had to reef early. Otherwise, we enjoyed this new concept of cruising immensely, and I jumped at the chance to go down any weekend.

* * *

We visited many of the little harbors and rivers dotted along the south coast and the IOW: Beaulieu, Cowes, Ryde, Lymington, Yarmouth, Newtown Creek, and Portsmouth. They ranged from completely deserted mud flats to bustling small towns with lots of restaurants and shopping. Most were a day's sail, if tides and wind were calculated properly. We could leave in the morning and be safely docked by midday. Beaulieu was our favorite and it didn't hurt that it was the closest, taking but a couple of hours to get there.

The Beaulieu River was actually several attractions in one. The river itself was and still is undeveloped on both sides, all the way to the little town of Beaulieu at its head. The town is the site for the National Motor Museum, a world-class collection of vehicles of all kinds and ages. Founded by Lord Montagu in the '50s, it now holds National Museum status, reflecting its importance to the U.K.'s motoring industry. Also on the grounds are the Beaulieu Abbey, the stunning Beaulieu Palace House, huge and beautiful gardens, and a monorail that encircles the entire facility. It is a fantastic place to visit. Like many of the Royal Family who own castles and grand estates, the Montagus have had to open their home to the public to help cover the immense cost of maintaining such a property.

We usually got a slip at Buckler's Hard Marina, which was about midway up the total length of the river. We would walk a couple of miles to the town of Beaulieu along the incredibly beautiful Beaulieu River. It is hard to describe the scenery along this stretch of river, being completely unspoiled and teeming with birds of all kinds. There were a couple of grand homes along the banks, but mostly it was pasture land on either side. This walk on a sunny summer day was pure magic.

Buckler's Hard was in itself a wonderful place. The inhabitants of this tiny hamlet used to build ships in the 18th century. Two rows of tiny Georgian cottages flank the main ship-building site, which was positioned on a slope directly into the river so that when completed, ships could easily be moved to the water and floated. There was a great museum explaining the activities from hundreds of years ago, and an excellent little hotel and restaurant called the Master Builder's House Hotel. You could take a tour of the little cottages and get a sense of what life was like almost 300 years earlier. It oozed charm from every pore. At 5' 9", I am not a tall person, but had to duck under all of the doorways in these small homes!

When I was about 16 years old and something of an athlete, we were on the docks in Beaulieu Marina as a 40' cruising yacht was coming into her berth. Having misjudged the tide pushing from behind, she was coming in far too fast (about 3 knots) and was going to smash into the dock pretty hard. I foolishly jumped in front of her, grabbed the stainless steel pulpit that extended past her bow several feet, and tried to slow her down. To say I was shocked at how little effect my efforts had would be an understatement. She crashed into the wooden dock with a hard crunch, leaving a big dent in the dock's lumber as well as a good scratch in her bow. She was lucky the dock wasn't concrete or didn't have a steel cap! It gave me the first real idea of how much power and inertia a boat in motion has. My dad generously said I'd helped slow her down, but I don't think so.

It is easy to see why we found this river to be such an attraction and came here several times every summer. The marina started out as just a line of moorings strung between piles in the river, but became a huge marina facility with full services. I have not been back there in many years; I hope expansion and progress have not ruined it.

Another favorite for us was Newtown Creek. This picturesque little river was a bit further along the IOW coast and being a Nature Reserve, had no development or structures of any kind. While a lot of the U.K. is pretty built up, this was an area of peaceful quiet. We loved visiting and listening to the many birds that lived there. We have one or two spectacular sunset photos from our visits.

A little further southwest was the small harbor town of Yarmouth. A much busier place, it was the site of one of the funniest boating events I've ever witnessed. Behind the harbor entrance is a river that winds into the IOW countryside for several miles. A fairly major road crosses the river at the mouth of the Solent. Accessing the harbor and river behind requires the bridge to be raised, a common occurrence during the sailing season. The French are known for their daring sailing prowess, and they would occasionally come across the English Channel. Yarmouth was one of the first harbors they could stop at.

One blustery day, an older French yacht of about 30' in length was coming into Yarmouth Harbor. They apparently had no engine of any kind and were sculling, which is the process of pushing and pulling a single oar centered on the stern of the boat to provide forward motion.

It's a common (and effective) technique for smaller boats, but not for something that probably weighed at least 10,000 pounds. Working against this yacht was a wicked ebb tide, running at about 3 knots OUT of the harbor. The poor guy on the scull was sawing back and forth like a madman, barely making any progress, while a long line of autos was backed up on shore, waiting for the bridge to go down and allow them to continue on their way again.

The visitor moorings were on the other side of the bridge, so we (and a number of other boats) had a front-row view of this hilarious episode. I am sure there was much head-shaking from the Brits, who generally regarded the French as an inferior seagoing nation. When the poor guy finally managed to get his bow around the corner of the bridge and out of the main tide flow, there was a huge cheer from the assembled yachties. Some of the cynics offered more of a jeer than a cheer, but in any case, it was good fun to watch.

* * *

One of the remarkable things about the Solent was the variety of commercial traffic that traveled it. Southampton, at the top of the Solent, is the second-busiest commercial port in the U.K. As such, commercial shipping traffic was constant, with some truly behemoth ships passing through. There were also dozens of ferries that plied back and forth between the little towns along the coast on both sides. Many were drive-on, drive-off ferries that were pretty traditional in design, with displacement hulls. These ships were around 200' and moved at 10 to 15 knots. There were also ferries that went from the UK to various European ports and they were much larger. In addition, there were also hydrofoil ferries around 70' that cruised at 25 to 30 knots. Finally, there were the hovercraft ferries that ran at 30+ knots and could drive right up on shore to dock. They were incredible machines, making a huge noise (although no wake) with a giant aircraft engine for forward thrust and another to keep the craft airborne.

These commercial ships cared not a whit about the hundreds, sometimes thousands, of pleasure yachts that frequented this rather small body of water. We had to keep a good lookout for the ferries, especially the fast ones, because they could be on you much faster than anticipated. While our best cruising speed was about 6 knots, all of these craft could go much faster – and were unpredictable. We learned the tracks of the ferries with time, but the tankers and container ships could be less predictable. If you were in their way, they let you know!

Another of our favorite locations was the town of Lymington. This was probably the largest of the little harbors we visited in terms of the town, with the marina being right at the bottom of the main street. It was a busy place, with ferries going to Yarmouth across the Solent as well as to Southampton and Cowes. The channel was narrow, so when a ferry came in, you had to be careful coming or going to make sure you gave it plenty of room. They could be very cranky about little yachts being in their way!

At the west end of the Solent was Hurst Castle on the north side and the Needles to the south. Like the White Cliffs of Dover, the Needles were made of the white chalk rock common along the south coast. They looked like little white teeth sticking up out of the water, with an old lighthouse (unmanned) at the end. It's a main landmark when going to or returning from the English Channel.

* * *

Every year since 1931, the Round Island Race is run counterclockwise around the Isle of Wight. The first race had 25 entries. In 2024, there were 939 entries, of which almost half had to retire due to wicked conditions of 40 knots and a nasty wind over tide going out the Needles at the start. There have been as many as 1,700 entries! The first yacht in 1931 did the 50-mile course in just shy of 10 hours and averaged about 5 knots. The current record by a Mod 70 trimaran is 2 hours and 22 minutes! That's an average of about 21 knots.

We never participated in this race as frankly, it was pretty intimidating. I imagine just figuring out which one of a couple dozen starts you would be in is a challenge in itself. We did travel 'round the island one perfect summer day, when the wind and tides were going in the right direction. I think it is fair to say that we would not have been far up the rankings, had it been a race day. But it was a stunning day, seeing the largely uninhabited back side of the IOW in sparkling sunshine and fair winds. You leave St. Catherine's Point and Bembridge to port before going back into the Solent at the east end. We were not very adventurous, and this felt like a great journey for us Solent hoppers.

* * *

English weather has a well-founded reputation for being miserable. While we lived in London, we experienced this all the time. Being on a small boat definitely prodded us "closer to nature." More than once, we went down to the boat, looking forward to a lovely weekend somewhere, only to be rained or blown out. Frankly, if you didn't go when it was raining, you would not have sailed much! As mentioned, the Solent was a pretty narrow piece of water, with strong tides twice a day. We had to plan our route to go with the tides as much as possible, since our little boats could only sail at about 6 knots. A 2- or 3-knot tide against us made for very slow going.

There is also a condition called "wind over tide," where the wind blows against the tide. This could produce truly ugly conditions, especially if both were strong. While the waves would not be particularly large by ocean standards, they could be wicked, sharp buggers that broke over the boat. Burying the bow was a normal occurrence. We were careful to try to avoid winds over about 20 knots. But occasionally, we'd get stuck somewhere, needing to get home on a Sunday afternoon, with no choice but to tough it out.

We had a "dodger," a bimini-like canvas cover over the main companionway that also provided protection at the forward end of the cockpit when the weather was bad. But the steering was always by tiller at the aft end of the cockpit, so whoever was there was out in the weather. As I got older, I'd take my turn at steering and give Dad a break. But it could be a pretty miserable place, with wind, rain, and spray whipping you in the face. Foul-weather gear at the time was not what it is today and Dad was super cheap, so I didn't have the good stuff. I don't think we ever saw more than a Force 8 (about 35 knots) and that was down to good planning and wisdom. While I was young enough to think it was still a little fun, my mom did not. So, Dad was smart about his route planning.

One other aspect of English sailing was the cold. Summer temps were frequently in the mid to high 60s that, when combined with 20 knots of very humid wind, could feel quite chilly. Nighttime temps dropped even further, and the fact that you were sitting in cold water with zero insulation in the boat hull meant for some cold nights. We all slept in good sleeping bags with our heads completely covered, except for our noses. We had a small propane heater Dad would turn on in the mornings to take the chill off. This warmed up the hull and created condensation on the hull walls. It was not unusual for me to wake up to water dripping on my face!

It did not take long to tire of the sailing characteristics of the Vega, and Dad was an obsessive boat buyer anyhow. So soon enough, we were looking for a new boat. Albin produced another boat called the Ballad that was 30', with a good fin keel and much better sailing characteristics. It was also a pretty boat, with a better level of finish. But the interior space was not a huge improvement over the Vega. While the main cabin was a bit wider and there was space for quarter-berths behind the main settees, the forepeak was about the same for me. At 13 years old, I had grown to 5' 9" and could not stand up straight any longer. The head was a bit bigger and there was a little more room around the galley, due to a bigger beam in the middle of the boat. However, we loved the sailing performance and enjoyed it every time we went out.

Speaking of Ballads, between 1967 and 1993, there was a competition among yachts with an IOR rating of 18 to 22 called the Half Ton Cup. This worked out to about 30' in length overall and was an open competition for all countries' yacht designs and brands. Some truly legendary designers showed off their designs for this regatta, including Paul Elvstrom, Doug Peterson, and Bruce Farr. The Ballad finished second in 1972 (I believe), which was an outstanding performance for a cruiser/racer. The yacht was a huge success, selling over 1,500 boats in a 12-year span.

Sailing and cruising was never my mom's thing. She much preferred fine hotels and five-star restaurants. But she gamely came along on the sailing adventures and I think eventually came to enjoy them. She was a really good cook, and used her imagination and creativity to come up with great meals using two low-temperature gas burners, limited prep space, and no refrigeration (until the last boat). She made do with ice boxes and coolers. She also didn't love the cold, but soldiered on when we were shivering in the mornings. Dad did make her coffee in bed most days. She loved the crewed and bareboat charters we – and she and Dad – took in warm places, like the BVI. The crewed charters were the best of course, where your every whim is catered to by an attentive and skilled crew.

Dad soon tired of the Ballad and a new boat was required. Did I mention there was little logic to his boat buying and selling? The next boat was a British-made Westerly Konsort. Westerly was known as a fairly budget British boat builder, but in the '80s started improving their quality and designs. It was actually a bit shorter than the Ballad, but offered what seemed like double the interior volume. The galley was significantly larger, which my mom appreciated. The forepeak was now a proper cabin, with enough headroom for me to stand up in (as long as I didn't move around much). Beam was carried further forward and aft as compared to the Ballad, so she felt a LOT larger. It was not quite as good a sailing boat, but the trade-off for the extra room was well worth it.

When I left for college in 1976, the Konsort was the boat my parents had, and so was the last one I have a good recollection of. It was a pretty good coastal cruiser for three adults. Like so many small yachts, she was advertised to sleep six. I'm sure friendlier folks would have been OK with that many aboard, but three was the limit for us. Mom and Dad did have the occasional sailing couples along for a weekend.

* * *

Living in London around this time was interesting, and not a little stressful. Northern Ireland had been occupied by the British Army in an effort to end the fighting that started in the late '60s between Catholics and Protestants. Between the two factions fighting each other and both of them fighting the British Army, there was a lot of bloodshed in Northern Ireland. That bloodshed spilled over into England through the efforts of the Irish Republican Army.

While gun violence in the U.K. was virtually unheard of, due to the fact that individual ownership of handguns is not allowed, the IRA brought their particular brand of terrorism to our doorstep. On Boxing Day (December 26), 1973, we were in our apartment with our downstairs neighbors visiting when we heard the unmistakable sound of a distant explosion. It turned out the IRA had planted a bomb packed with nails designed to cause maximum death and injury in a pub in Swiss Cottage, about three-quarters of a mile up the road from us. Dozens were maimed and injured. Two years later, the IRA placed a bomb in the lobby of the London Hilton, killing two and injuring 63. My dad's office at the time was in the building next door.

Since our school was a de facto outpost of the American government, bomb scares (and evacuations) at the school were pretty common.

It might sound like London would be a scary place to live during this time. We were encouraged to keep our eyes open and pay attention to untended packages or bags, particularly in public places and on public transport. But as a teenager, the events felt slightly detached from our daily lives. It is far scarier to live in a country with over 400 million guns today.

* * *

Dad got the bug again a few years later and upgraded to a Sadler 34. Sadler was the same builder that designed and built the very famous Contessa 26 and 32. They were high-quality blue ocean cruisers, even though they were not large. We had looked at the Contessa 26 when shopping for our first boat and admired the build quality and seagoing capabilities. Many 26s had crossed oceans and even circumnavigated, with a full keel, protected rudder, and classic lines from the '60s. She was not, however, a very big boat down below and was also quite expensive, so didn't make the cut. Dad couldn't stand up in her, which soon would have been a problem for us both.

Sadler wanted a more mainstream yacht and a cheaper one compared to the Contessa, so introduced the Sadler line, which ranged from 25'to 39". The 34 was kind of the next logical step for my parents, with a U-shaped galley, yet more interior space, and very handsome lines. While Dad had paid something like £3,500 for the Vega in 1970, the Sadler was around £60,000. He said he "made" money on all of his boats, which I guess in the fact that he sold them for more than he bought them, he did. But the Sadler was a huge jump up from the Konsort in every way. Boat costs go up exponentially with length and the 34 cost more to buy, berth, insure, maintain, and repair.

Dad was one of the first buyers of the 34 and had some real issues with the boat straight out of the factory. Any cruising boat is like a small home, with many of the same systems – and some that homes don't have, like a diesel engine. There was hot and cold pressurized water, a plumbed toilet and sink in the head, lighting, and a charging system for two different batteries (like an RV, one for the "house" and one for the engine), and propane for the stove and a heater. That doesn't count the sails, the mast and rigging, or a ton of lines and winches to control everything, which on a 34-footer were considerable.

He complained bitterly about the poor attention to detail and the lack of responsiveness from the factory. Once while they were sailing, he went below to find the cabin floor covered in water. Fearing the worst (a hole in the hull), he tasted the water and found it was fresh water, not salt. A fitting on the freshwater tank had not been tightened enough at the factory and the contents had filled the bilge, then the cabin. It was the kind of thing that drove him crazy and spoiled the enjoyment of a new boat.

In 1989, my parents decided to move to Colorado to be closer to their grandkids, and Dad's coastal cruising came to an end. After he moved to Colorado, his first boat was an Ericson 25, a proper "little yacht" that turned out to be too large to tow around in a mountainous state. After that, his trailerable boats got smaller and more manageable, but I think he always missed having a real yacht.

Chapter Four

Racing at 9,000'

I moved to Denver, after graduating from high school in 1976, to attend the University of Denver. DU was founded in 1864, predating Colorado becoming a state by 12 years. It also beat what is now Colorado State University by six years. The campus is a few miles from downtown Denver on the major north/south highway, I-25. There are some original buildings, but most of the campus was updated in the '90s, thanks to a ton of investment. It is renowned for its business and accounting programs. I started in Psychology and changed to Environmental Science after one year, realizing that Psychology required a lot of schooling and the first few years were not going to be all that interesting. Environmental Science was a lot more interesting but not all that marketable, unless one wanted to go on to get an advanced degree.

I spent the first three years in the dorms, two of them as a Resident Assistant (RA). It was a way to get free room and board, although dealing with immature and/or crazy students could sometimes be a pain. I had a guy on my floor my junior year who was also named Mike. He seemed to have a death wish, as he got himself into all kinds of trouble. His buddy had a Jeep, and they were doing donuts in the parking lot one afternoon. Mike was hanging off the roll bar, and pulled hard to the inside in one turn – and pulled the Jeep over on top of himself. He managed to only get some bumps and bruises, but a seriously pissed-off friend.

In the dorm, he seemed to have a sixth sense about how far he could go and not get caught. It was a constant frustration to me that I couldn't catch him in the act of doing something. Late one night, I heard a rustling in the hallway and peeked out my door. Our dorms were arranged in a big rectangle, so there were two long hallways and two short ones, with the bathrooms, laundry, and elevators in the middle. I couldn't see anything, but someone was definitely out there struggling with something heavy.

I tip-toed out, so I could look down the long hallway, and found Mike wrestling a 30-gallon trash full of water against his friend's door (Jeep guy). Busted! The look on his face was priceless. Obviously, 30 gallons of water in a small dorm room would have made a huge mess, and run down to the floors below. This, on top of some other transgressions, was the end and he was asked to leave the dorm. I ran into him years later and he had become a lawyer, so at some point he got his act together.

* * *

I graduated from DU in the summer of 1980. About the same time, a small ad popped up in The Clarion, the DU newspaper. This was before digital anything, so newspaper ads were the way to go. It was a guy with a J-24 looking for crew for the summer at Lake Dillon. I had not been on a sailboat since leaving the UK, so I called him up. Dick Fell was a generous skipper and a good sailor. Little did I know that my relationship with the J-24 was to become one of the greatest in my sailing life.

Lake Dillon is a roughly 5,000-acre reservoir about 60 miles west of Denver, surrounded by mountains on all sides. The original town of Dillon is still at the bottom of the very deep lake, which is about 300 feet at its deepest. Anchoring is a bad idea not only because of the depth, but because the original forest is still down there, ready to take your anchor away from you! A new town of Dillon was built, with the town of Frisco more or less at the other end. The ski resort of Keystone is just up the valley in one direction and Breckenridge in another. At 9,000 feet elevation, it is one of the highest lakes in the U.S. Our stunning views included most of Breckenridge's ski mountains, which retained snow for much of the summer.

Dick Fell was an airline pilot and the boat was called Blue Side Down. This is a riff on the pilot's expression to "Keep the Blue Side Up" which, if you're in an airplane, is probably a good thing! Keeping the blue side down is also a good thing when you're in a boat. As trimmer, my role was to get the big genoa around the boat. It was tricky, and required good timing and communication with the skipper. It also required some strength and while I was fit, I was hardly a muscular guy. But I did have a good sense of how to trim a sail and we quickly gelled as a crew.

The J-24 is a particularly popular boat, having sold over 5,500 worldwide. It is sailed with a blade jib, a smallish main, and a large overlapping genoa. Very rarely is the blade jib used, even in high winds. It weighs about 3,000 pounds and has a small keel of 900 pounds. It can be towed fairly easily by a small truck or an SUV.

It is very sensitive to weight placement and, like most modern designs with fin keels, likes to be sailed pretty flat. It has a racing crew weight limit of 400 kilograms or 882 pounds. This meant a crew of four or five, if you had some smaller people. Crew has to move side to side with each tack, and those in the middle do not have it good. The foredeck person can step around the mast. The trimmer and skipper step across the cockpit. The sewer and #5 have to slide under the boom. This takes some agility and timing.

As the boat starts to tack, you lean back from your hiking position on the rail and grab the boom. As the boat goes through the tack, you heave yourself under the boom, swing your legs around, and get back on the rail. As you can imagine, there is lots of opportunity for scratches and bruises; there was frequently a "best bruise" contest at big regattas. Lots of these middle positions were crewed by women, so there was no lack of enthusiasm by the mostly male crowd to see bruised butts and thighs. Some of them were truly wince-inducing!

Crews were weighed before big regattas, which can lead to some funny situations. Before a big regatta on Lake Dillon, we were over by a few pounds. Generally, you wanted as much weight as possible in the strong winds that were typical. I was at my promised weight of

172 pounds. So, the big guy who'd had a bit too much fun the night before had to don his foul-weather gear and run around for an hour to shed his extra weight.

We won the J-24 fleet the summers of '80 and '81 against a competitive fleet of 18 to 25 boats. We also went to the SW Regionals in Dallas, Texas, one year and finished seventh against 42 boats and some truly tough competition, including Paul Foerster, a (future) three-time Olympic medalist.

* * *

Sixteen years later, I would sail on Blue Side Down again, then owned by Judge Dave Helmer, another very nice guy with a killer instinct on the water. Judge Helmer was the local county judge; a lot of jokes were made about making sure you didn't beat him, in case you ended up before his bench someday.

It is hard to do justice to the setting. The lake at 9,000' elevation is obviously already way up there, but the surrounding peaks reached to 13,000' and higher. The air was as clean and clear as can be, with no pollution and few clouds in the summertime. The water was a rich, deep blue, reflecting the sky. Even though the water was also crystal clear, there was no bottom to lighten the color: it just looked dark and endless. To the south was South Park (yes, of the TV show fame), a large flat area of high plains that heated up during the day and pulled air over Hoosier Pass and up the Dillon valley.

The lake would usually be dead calm until about 11:30 a.m., when the thermals would start. Usually by noon or 12:30, you'd have a steady 15 to 20 knots for the rest of the afternoon. Occasionally, a thunderstorm would come over the mountains and either suck all the air out of the lake or provide some excitement in the form of very high winds. I got caught out on a J-24 one day with the main up, and we were knocked so far over I could see the keel out of the water! I was hanging onto the windward rail for dear life. I found out later the on-water weather station recorded 62 mph, about 52 knots.

Winds could also get turned inside out. Another day on a J-24 with one of my favorite skippers, Frank K, we were leading the race. We had turned the leeward mark, had the spinnaker up, and were heading back upwind. All eyes were in the boat at the time trying to get everything sorted out, except Frank's. He calmly said, "Hey guys, we need to get the spinnaker down right away." Looking up, we saw the whole fleet was bearing down on us with THEIR spinnakers up! "You've got about five seconds." Then, quietly counted it down, "Five, four, three, two, one." We managed to get the chute down without too much fuss but needless to say, the fleet reduced our lead dramatically. I loved Frank.

In the summer of 1982, I married Lili, whom I had met at DU. We went on a spectacular honeymoon, which included a week in Miami with her parents, a couple of weeks in London (and a week on my parents cruising boat), a few days in Paris and Madrid, and a week with her Uncle in Logrono in northern Spain. It was an amazing trip of over five weeks.

* * *

We had a funny boating experience in Miami. Lili was not a sailor, but she was game to give it a try. We rented an Ensign from a rental place on Biscayne Bay, right in front of the skyline of Miami. The Ensign is a very old design, with a deep, full-length keel, keel hung rudder, a huge cockpit that didn't drain, and a small cuddy with no accommodation. It was a good boat for a rental, as it was overbuilt and very tough. I was to become very familiar with these boats on Lake Dillon a few years later.

It was a stunning South Florida day, about 85 degrees, with bright sun and steady winds from the east blowing across the bay. It had been a couple of years since I had left Blue Side Down and I was enjoying the day. The boat had no engine, so we had to tack up a narrow channel to get away from the rental place, and it was not going well. The boat's sails were old and saggy, and her bottom was not clean – which was not conducive to tacking up a tight channel.

We finally got out into the bay and we were really enjoying ourselves. Lili was laying down on the leeward bench, sunning herself. We were well heeled over on a beam reach, parallel to the shore and approaching the city center. I wasn't paying particular attention and realized suddenly that we were surrounded by grass! I ordered a fast tack, which of course changed the depth of the boat. While we were heeling, the keel wasn't very deep, but once we tried to tack, the keel went straight up and down, and immediately dug into the soft bottom, bringing us to a screeching halt. And, of course, the wind was blowing us further into the shallow area.

I tried to sheet in again and heel the boat over, but she was having none of it. We were stuck. We were not in swimsuits, but I jumped in the water, assuming the bottom was soft, and tried to pull her off, backing up against the wind. The Ensign is not a light boat, I did not have good traction and frankly, I was figuratively and literally in over my head. This was way before cell phones, so we had no way to contact the rental place.

After struggling for probably an hour, a power boater saw me in the water and came over to offer help. I handed them the line and hopped back on board the Ensign. With me hanging on the end of the boom to heel the boat over, they pulled us clear. But unfortunately, they got some of the grass wound around their prop and ended up getting stuck themselves!

At this point, I didn't see any way we could offer assistance in return, so I yelled an apology and we headed back to the rental place. I felt terrible leaving them there, and they probably cursed us for needing to be helped in the first place. We had only rented for four hours and barely made it back in time. I was to return to Biscayne Bay many years later under very different circumstances. This was the beginning of our honeymoon, so there was lots to look forward to and enjoy.

* * *

Dad's first boat in 1989 in Colorado was an Ericson 25, a proper little yacht with a full teak interior of main cabin, small head compartment, and forepeak. It was a handsome boat as well. It had a swinging centerboard, useful when towing but not much use over about 15 knots. We tried racing her at Dillon, but found out quickly that she was not appropriate for the stronger winds found there.

There were active fleets of J-24s, Santana 22s, and Ensigns, so we decided to buy a Santana 22 and go one-design racing. This proved to be a great decision. The S-22 and Ensign had about the same PHRF rating, so the two fleets usually started together. As we found out later, the Commodore of the Club was a Santana 22 owner, and he didn't think the Ensign should have a better rating than his boat, so all S-22's at Dillon got a very favorable rating. In every other fleet in the country, the boat carried a much lower rating.

The S-22 was an old design from the early '60s, with a small cabin and huge non-foil shaped keel. The total weight of the boat was about 2,700 pounds, with almost half of that in the keel. That made it very stable for the high winds we frequently had on Lake Dillon. There was a huge 150% overlapping genoa and a relatively small main. We sailed with a traditional symmetrical spinnaker of about 350 square feet.

There were five or six active S-22s and eight to ten Ensigns, several of which were very well sailed. This meant a pretty busy start line most weekends, with 14 to 15 boats. One of the most notable Ensigns was NIGYSOB or "Now I've Got You, You Son Of A Bitch," a funny and provocative name for a boat if ever there was one. NIGYSOB was skippered by Skip N, an excellent sailor who had done very well with his Ensign in the club and at the national level. Skip was not afraid to use the racing rules as a sword and not a shield, and his on-water tantrums were legendary. Beating Skip head-to-head was something to be proud of and it was to take a couple of years before I did so.

Our first full season after buying the boat started off well enough, but we were making dumb mistakes and struggling to find consistency. As the year went on, our results got worse instead of better. Toward the end of the season, after a particularly bad day, I was wondering aloud why we seemed so slow and stuck my hand in the water to feel the hull bottom. There were blisters all over it. When we bought the boat, the previous owner had painted the bottom with car paint. We didn't know that would never hold up when left in the water all summer. He had been dry sailing the boat, so never had a problem. It was a stupid mistake. We pulled the boat immediately, for fear water would get under the paint and damage the fiberglass hull. It was the end of our first year's racing. That winter, we got a proper racing bottom done by our local shop.

The other change we made was that I became skipper. My dad was not really enjoying being skipper and was not as serious as I was, which created some bad blood between us. So, he decided to stay on shore and play with the grandkids, and let me race. I proceeded to work on getting regular crew for the summer, knowing that was a key to winning. I also made some other changes to the rigging to make trimming sails easier and faster. My goal was to win the S-22 Summer Series. All boats and classes also competed for the Overall Championship under the PHRF handicapping system. This handicap theoretically allowed fast and slow boats to compete head to head.

One of the most important keys to our success was my foredeck, Craig R. The year before, I'd picked his name off the crew bulletin board at the yacht club, and he'd proven to be the perfect Dillion foredeck: not too big (too much weight forward is bad), strong and agile, and most importantly, calm under pressure. Things could get hairy with changing conditions, and having someone forward who didn't get flustered was super important. Plus, the foredeck of a small racing boat is not a very safe place. It's small, it moves around a lot, and if you stumble or fall, you are almost certainly going overboard into the very cold waters of Lake Dillon. (The water temp rarely got above 50°, even at the end of the season.) He was from back east and worked at Vail ski area, and had a lot of sailing experience. Having another experienced guy on board helped with our success.

I lined up a good group of people. Even though they weren't exactly the same every weekend, we were never short of a crew of four, which was ideal. And we had enough consistency that we were not starting over with newbies every weekend. There was Manny and

Erik, and Sue and Rick, who were real characters. They had been married for many years, and sailed together and apart for much of that time. Both of them were good sailors. I felt lucky to have them on board, when they could make it. They were not, however, warm and fuzzy while on the boat and frequently fought bitterly. They were as gentle and loving as could be on shore, after the racing had finished. I asked them about this, and they said racing was racing and stayed on the water. I thought it was odd they would continue to sail together, but they seemed perfectly happy with the arrangement.

Sue was a competitive age-group swimmer, so was fit and strong, and usually wore her hair in a long ponytail. We were in the midst of a high-tension situation, the specifics of which aren't important. I asked Rick to pull on a bunch of mainsheet, which was attached in the middle of the boom, not at the end. He didn't notice that Sue's ponytail was in the mainsheet block, so as he pulled on the line, her head was yanked into the boom. Of course, feeling resistance, he pulled harder, and smacked his wife's head good and hard into the boom. Sue was yelling for him to let go, but in the general noise and excitement, he hadn't heard her. Wow, was she mad, and let him have it with both barrels! This was the one time anger on the boat carried over to the bar later in the evening.

* * *

My dad bought a condo on Buffalo Mountain, outside Silverthorne. This saved having to get a condo or hotel room for the weekend and allowed us a base of operations. The condo was at 10,000' elevation, up a very windy road and surrounded by National Forest land. There were great hiking trails in several directions, including to Lily Pad Lake, about a 90-minute hike up Buffalo Mountain. It was a spectacular setting, with amazing mountain views in several directions. One could almost see the lake in the distance. There were two real bedrooms plus a loft and three bathrooms, plus Grandma and Grandpa, and by this time the EX and I had 2 kids so there was plenty of space for all of us. The EX and the kids would hang out at the condo or do things in town while I sailed. It was a great arrangement.

Having a place to stay also gave us more flexibility in terms of traveling to Denver, which on a good day was about a 75-minute drive. Most of it was on notorious I-70, which went through Eisenhower Tunnel, the highest tunnel in the U.S. at 11,158' elevation. Traffic on Sunday afternoons was almost always bad, stretching the drive to two hours at times. So, we either tried to wait until later or leave first thing on Monday.

Weather at 10,000' in the Colorado mountains could be interesting. We once had 4" of snow on the 4th of July! Frisco used to have a great fireworks display over Lake Dillon and another year it was snowed out! Not something you hear very often. Days were usually warm, rarely over 80°, and nights were cool, frequently in the 40s and 50s.

Having a regular crew helped us get better. We knew the boat was fast, so needed to nail the crew work. By the end of the Summer Series, we had easily won the S-22 fleet, and ended up 11th overall in PHRF out of 47 boats. There were usually two races each day on Saturday and Sunday. For some reason, the S-22s didn't race the second race on Sunday, so we were immediately at a disadvantage in the overall, throwing away something like ten races each season. Resentment in the S-22 fleet started right away, with my much more thorough and prepared approach to racing.

For instance, our crew sat on the side deck to maximize our hiking leverage and also keep weight centered in the boat, like any good small racing keel boat should. Most S-22s we raced against kept all their crew in the cockpit. This was safer and dryer, but it dragged the stern of the boat down, making it slower.

The next season, I set our sights on the overall PHRF Championship, meaning we had to race both races on Sunday. All the other S-22s went in Sunday afternoon, so this pitted us against just the Ensigns, which was an interesting situation. Skip, recognizing that I was serious about beating him, did a lot of yelling at me that summer. We had some epic battles on Sunday afternoons! He had finished second overall the year before behind Blue Side Down in the overall.

I once again easily won the S-22 fleet, throwing out firsts for the series. We ended up third overall out of 47 total boats, beaten by two J-24s. Dave H on Blue Side Down was fifth and the great Skip Nitchie with NIGYSOB was fourth, one place behind us! I have to say it was probably the most satisfying result of my whole racing career. Not because Skip was a screamer on the racecourse, but because he was a really good sailor and beating him meant something. He did congratulate me, but I think I saw some clenched teeth.

* * *

Dillon Yacht Club (DYC) also ran other events, some of which we had success in as well. Probably the premier regatta in the state was the Dillon Open, which usually runs late in August. DYC ran a great regatta, with legendary parties sponsored by Mount Gay Rum, a popular supporter of sailing regattas all over the world. Their bright red hats are recognizable everywhere. Besides the large local fleet, this attracted boats from all over the state and the region. It was cool to see sometimes close to 100 boats on our little lake! It was not uncommon for larger classes to run their regional or national events alongside the regular racing. This attracted top-notch sailors from all over the country. The S-22s raced as a class in this regatta; some would bring in "ringers" for this regatta, since it was so prestigious. We finished second, first, and second in class in '94, '95 and '96.

DYC also ran a Frostbite Series in the fall with some of the best winds of the year, as they tended to calm down a little. In '95, we finished fourth behind Blue Side Down, NYGISOB, and a Star, an interesting mix of PHRF boats! There were 22 boats sailing that one. Then in '96, we improved one place to third, behind (once again) Blue Side Down and a different Ensign, with 19 boats. (NYGISOB was not sailing that regatta.)

DYC also ran a Single-Handed Race, which led to one of the more frantic sailing events of my life. The S-22 was not really set up for single-handed sailing, with the genoa sheet winches well forward in the cockpit and the helm aft. The main sheet control was in the middle of the boom and the other sail controls (traveler and backstay tension) were aft, all easily reached from the helm position. With a 150% genoa, being able to get to the winches was critical, so it was a bit of a scramble to tack the genoa around, change the traveler location, adjust the backstay, etc.

I was doing reasonably well in typical Dillon conditions – crystal clear blue skies with the occasional white puffy cloud and about 15 to 20 knots of breeze. After rounding the leeward mark, the tiller came away in my hand. It literally snapped at the base! Fortunately, the boat rounded up into the wind, dumping all power from the sails, but here I was with no way to steer the boat! I got the sails down without too much trouble and examined my problem.

The tiller had broken at the base where it was bolted through the large stainless-steel rudder stock. I found some tools to remove the old stump of the tiller, then lashed what was left into the bracket, giving me at least some control to get back to the dock. It all turned out OK, but it was a pretty horrible feeling to pull on the tiller and have it rip apart like that!

While some of the other S-22 owners were happy to see one of their own compete on the bigger stage, there was a fair amount of resentment that I had come in and ruined their quiet, laid-back racing fleet. Frankly, winning by miles was not all that much fun, so I decided to sell the boat. The S-22 boats were mostly owned by older folks and as they aged out of racing, the fleet kind of fell apart. I believe there is only one boat left up there now. Shame…

Chapter Five

1996 Miami Midwinters – Rubbing Elbows with Terry Hutchinson

This is a log of the J-24 Midwinter Championship in Miami, Florida, January 7–12, 1996. I went with ChuckWagon, owned by Peter W. The other members of our team included Luther T, a chiropractor from Breckenridge, who sailed with Dave H on Blue Side Down (the top J-24 at Dillon for many years); Steve T, who generally had a lot of sailing experience, including an Olympic Laser campaign; Bob H, who went by "Bobbo," who had been around the Dillon scene and done a number of big regattas; and Peter, who had also been around the Colorado sailing scene for a lot of years, and taken ChuckWagon to several big events and done well. The boat was actually a former J-24 World Champion, having won with a group of pros in a previous year.

I flew in with Luther, going through Minneapolis on Northwest Airlines. We got in quite late on Friday, January 5th. Luther was an enjoyable traveling companion who had that ability to talk to anyone about anything, any time! I stayed with Lisa W, a friend of the family. She had a very nice house about two miles from the marina the regatta sailed out of. Peter had towed the boat from Colorado and was there when we arrived.

Saturday, January 6

The boats had to be put in at Crandon Marina, about 6 miles out on the Key of Biscayne. I had no car, so I used Lisa's bike, which was just fine except that it was a lot further in reality than on the map!

I got there huffing and puffing, and had already had my workout for the day. Peter's tow car was a bright red '76 Cadillac Sedan DeVille Coupe, which must have been the largest production car made since the '30s. A small family could live in this thing, and it had a modest (sarcasm) 500 cubic inch motor. What a tank!

There were a number of boat details that needed to be taken care of, including a sprucing up of the bottom, charging of the battery, sail measurement and check-in, and crew weigh-in. The crew weight limit was 880 pounds, or 176 pounds per person with five crew. Peter and I spent several hours sanding and polishing the bottom (this was SOP at every regatta), while Luther and Bob did most of the other stuff. Frank K was basically having to redo his bottom, but his brother Jim was done by midafternoon. Frank's boat was called "Do Not Play on or Around This Dumpster," or just "The Dumpster" for short. The three of us were the Colorado contingent.

When we put the mast up, the backstay was somehow about 4" short, which we couldn't figure out – until Luther thought that he may have put the forestay in the wrong hole at the top of the mast. Oops. We ran out of daylight before we were able to confirm this, so we took off to see if we could find Steve, who had not come in yet, and get a new outhaul for the boom. (Both were taken care of expeditiously.)

We bought beer and got a recommendation on a great little Greek restaurant that wasn't cheap, but everyone's meals seemed to be very good. (I know mine was!) Peter treated us to a bottle of wine for our efforts, which was generous considering all the freebees the crew got for the regatta, including a huge breakfast (eggs, bacon, sausage, toasted bagels, and OJ) every day of racing, three dinners, and parties with free Brugal Rum, the sponsor of the event.

It was a tough group, each good in their own right. Steve was probably the most experienced overall, which is why he would be calling tactics. Luther trimmed and called tactics on Blue Side Down, and Peter had been campaigning a J for a while. Bob had been one of the top foredeck guys for years on Dillon. I thought I would fit in, in that I was general enough to fill the cracks wherever it was needed. My official title was "sewer," meaning I handled getting the spinnaker in and out of the hatch, and adding rail meat (weight on the rail to balance the boat). It was a good balance of skills and personalities, which I was convinced made for great crews and fast boats. We knew we had good boat speed. ChuckWagon was a former World Champion, after all!

We were on Biscayne Bay, just in front of the Miami skyline, protected from the ocean by barrier islands. It was quite shallow and high winds could kick up a really nasty short chop. It made for very wet upwind legs and scary down winds. It was easy to plow into the wave in front when going fast with the chute up.

Most of the top guys were there: Chris Larson, multiple World and National Champion in various classes, including the J-24, a Pan Am Games Gold Medal, Multiple Match Racing events, and Rolex Yachtsman of the Year. Chris Snow, multiple J-24 National and World Championships as well as several other classes, including the J-70 in 2018. Terry Hutchinson, multiple World and National Champion in a variety of boats, including the TP52, J-24, and Farr 40; Terry was the president of the American Magic America's Cup syndicate and involved in five previous AC campaigns, all winners. Brad Read, College Sailor of the Year, three-time J-24 World Champion, two-time J-24 North American Champion. Mark Laura, J-24 North American Champion, Thistle Midwinters, etc., on Frank K's boat. There were also others I wasn't familiar with. The J-24 class attracted the best sailors in the world. On Sunday, we got everything perfect and practiced a lot. I was a bit nervous about doing everything as smoothly as these top-notch guys were used to.

Sunday, January 7

The other four stayed with a work colleague of Peter's out by Crandon Marina. They told me to be ready by 8:00 a.m. At about 1:30, Bob finally showed up! We got down to the boat and went out for some practice. The mechanics seemed to be pretty well down, but we struggled with boat speed. Steve had some new ideas that Peter was not familiar with, and we tried several different ways to increase the speed. We had the genoa up in 20+ knots, which was probably too much breeze for the sail. The waves were pretty big and irregular, so it was hard to feel like we had a groove. We got to speed test with a couple other boats and it was apparent that the jib was the better way to go. (The J-24 has either a large overlapping genoa or blade jib, a standard main, and spinnaker.)

We turned around and threw the chute, which with the big waves was quite a thrill! We were surfing wildly down the fronts of waves and trying to go across the face of them like a surfer. Unfortunately, we didn't know how fast we were going, but I would guess pushing 20 knots anyhow. It was certainly the fastest I've ever gone in a sailboat! We absolutely screamed past a cruiser under his working jib, who must have thought we were crazy. At one point, we went fast enough to bury the bow in the wave in front of us. This was fun for those of us in the back, but not so much fun for Bob, who was changing jibs on the bow; he was drenched with white water.

A big squall arrived and we headed in, not knowing exactly where we were going. Unfortunately, the channel was poorly marked, and we went aground. A support boat came over and pulled us off. I was cold and soaked to the skin after repeated drenching by waves and Bob was also shivering, so we were glad to hear they had showers. The only problem was, there were no towels. We made do with t- shorts and sweatshirts. Dinner was great: barbecued ribs and chicken, and free rum courtesy of the main sponsor. We ripped off our port sponsor sticker during the wild downwind, that's how crazy it had been.

I didn't really feel prepared to do battle with some of the world's best the next day, but Steve and Luther seemed confident. I had slipped and whacked my elbow on the dock earlier in the day, so had a tender 3" bruise and two sore palms. The forecast for Monday was very windy (20-30 knots) and only mid 50s for the highs - so much for sunny and warm Miami!

Later that night, Lisa and I had a bit of excitement when a transformer on the pole behind her house went off like a cannon around 11:15 p.m. We were both scared out of bed. Poor Lisa was glad to have me around, as she was terrified that it had something to do with the electrical work she was having done in her house. Once we figured out what the noise was, I reassured her the house was not going to catch on fire, and we once again called it a night.

Monday, January 8

What a day. As promised, it dawned clear, but quite cold and blustery. I walked down to the marina and bought some ugly rubber boots, because I knew if the wind was indeed going to blow, I was going to be wet all day. The closer you are to the front of the boat, the colder and wetter it gets. My boots were $16.99 specials from the inappropriately named Crook and Crook. The wind was blowing from the land out to sea, so we were protected a bit in the marina, but it felt like it was in the mid to high teens. The temperature at this time wasn't much over 40°. As predicted, the high for the day was in the mid 50s.

There were 38 boats at the regatta. We pushed off at about 9:00 a.m. (first gun was supposed to be at 9:50) and followed the procession of boats out. The committee boat was a huge power boat, probably 55'. As we got further from land, the wind built steadily and the waves got bigger. We threw the chute for practice, and then the fun really began.

We started toward the west a little after 10:00; the wind was solidly around 20 knots with higher gusts. We had two general recalls, meaning so many boats were over early, they called the whole fleet back as opposed to calling out individual boats. The first start we were in good shape – the second, not so good. Peter struggled to trust the crew to sight the line, and he was too worried about being over early. The line was really too long, but they were trying to prevent the problems many of the big regattas had with too many recalls. On the third start they flew a black flag, meaning that anyone over was immediately DSQ'd, which should have discouraged anyone from being too aggressive.

We again had a pretty good start, with good speed and reasonably clear air. We were about a third of the way down the line. We had to tack a couple of times to get a clear lane which hurt us, and were struggling to get in a groove in the very lumpy seas and high wind. We were taking big waves over the bow, and Bob and I were getting drenched, again. I was wearing every piece of clothing I'd brought, including eight layers on the top and three on the bottom. I was warm, but my foul weather gear was not up to the task of keeping me dry. By the end of the day, I was soaked to my skin, again! The 65° water temperature was actually quite a bit warmer than the air temp, which was in the low 50s.

We got to the windward mark, which was a gate with two marks spread about 50 yards apart – a good idea in a big fleet. It added a strategic decision point as to which way to go. We had a good spinnaker set, but rounded up hard a couple of times. When we did finally get going, we were really screaming downwind and catching other boats in the process. We were probably in the bottom third of the fleet at this time. There were a couple of pretty good broaches on other boats and several boats just stuck with the jib, even downwind.

The leeward mark was also a gate. You had to pick which mark was closest and/or gave you the best side of the course going back upwind. We had an absolutely great takedown, even though the wind was continuing to build. Going back to windward, we began moving better. Dumpster (Frank K's boat, with Mark Laura steering) was right in front of us, and they took a long tack out to the left, which we didn't think was the way to go. We stayed more middle and ended up at about the same relative position to each other 15 minutes later. However, we had both picked up a bunch of positions. (We found out later that we went from 28th to 17th on this leg.)

This time, our set was not quite so good: we dunked the chute in the water, which stopped us immediately. It filled up and then tore down one of the major seams. We brought it back on board in two pieces. Steve thought we could put up the genny and go wing on wing, which struck me as a crazy thing to try at the point. We messed with that for several minutes, during which Bob ended up with a tangle on the bow, and we were going slowly.

A Boat Sinks

A couple of boats in front of us did wild broaches and swamped with water, including Jim K. We went to the aid of one of them. Actually, there was some talk that it might help our chances in the standings if we went to their aid, which I thought was a bit self-serving. One of the boats looked to be turning turtle and two people were in the water. Fortunately, the water was quite warm, even if it was frothy from the wind, which was still building. We picked them up and hung around while the rest of the crew tried to get the boat moving again. They had taken on a bunch of water and the boat was very sluggish. We tried to decide whether we should go in or try to finish. We decided to finish, and put the jib back up.

Meanwhile, Doghouse had all five crew in the water, and the boat was obviously sinking. The support boat was on hand and pulled them all free. I was on the rail hiking out, and got a series of pictures of the boat going down. They came out OK, but it was an old film underwater disposable camera, so not good quality. I took a picture of the boat about two-thirds in the water with Jim clearly hanging on, and gave it to him a couple months later. I am not sure he appreciated it very much.

That afternoon, Jim K, the owner of Doghouse, hired a diving crew to raise the boat with air bags, and it was towed back to the marina. He rented industrial dehumidifiers to dry out the interior of the boat overnight and was at the start line the next day. Nice to have a large disposable income!

We managed to pick off two rear-enders and actually didn't finish DFL, 28th at the finish line. This was pretty amazing because we must have spent at least 15 minutes helping the other boat and deciding whether we were going to continue or not. The wind was solidly in the low 30s by now, as the spray from waves was being blown flat. The waves were nasty sharp-edged buggers that were throwing huge lapful's of water at Bob and me every time we came down. I was soaked, as was Bob, and we were both f---ing cold.

We made our way back to the marina, which was a hard slog to weather. We left the jib up, only to realize later that we had torn a seam on it as well. When we got in, we took a quick shower, had lunch, and picked up some stuff at West Marine. All the guys you would expect to do well did: Hutchinson, Read, Johnstone, Snow, and Larson. Everyone but Mark Laura had a good day. I ended my day with a delicious dinner with Lisa at a local fish restaurant.

Tuesday, January 9

The day dawned cold, clear, and not so windy. The temperature at 8:00 a.m. was about 40°. I was not looking forward to another chilly day, but luckily I had dried all my clothes in Lisa's dryer. The guys came by to pick me up about 7:45, and we got away from the dock around 9:00-ish. Crew work and sail handling were very good; I doubt any boat in the regatta was consistently better. The wild stuff on Lake Dillon had been good training. (To be honest, I can't remember how we took care of the torn sails, whether we repaired them or borrowed extras from other boats.)

We had a long sail out to the course, which was several miles from the marina. The wind was 8 to 10 knots, the temperature was climbing quickly, and seas were 1 to 2 feet – so much nicer conditions than on Monday!

We had two general recalls before getting in a good start. We were just short of the line, but had good speed. We got buried quickly and ended up having to make several extra tacks, which hurt us badly. While we were showing decent speed, any extra maneuvering was deadly and could make a giant difference in placing. We ended up in the bottom half of the pack at the windward mark and looked pretty bad.

We picked up a couple of boats on the downwind, but when we turned to go back upwind, we picked the wrong side of the course and ended up well down. The next downwind had a big course change and it appeared that most of the fleet missed it, as they did a 90-degree turn and headed 30 degrees high of the mark. Steve caught the change, and we took a much more direct course in a slowly dying breeze. We ended up passing a bunch of boats to finish 19th. We were about fifth from the back (out of 38!) when we rounded the last windward mark, so we picked up almost half the fleet on one leg!

The wind was shifting left (south) as the cold front passed through, and the prevailing winds seem to be taking over. We saw some dolphins before the race, which was kind of cool for us Colorado boys! In the second race, we had two general recalls, both of which were good starts for us. The third was still pretty good, but unless you had room to leeward and were able to point up, you would quickly be "shot out the back," as they say. We again had to pick our way through the pack with lots of chopped-up wind, and we ended up in the bottom third again.

The downwind was uneventful, but we picked up a couple of boats. The wind was now in the 5-knot range, but relatively steady. Steve decided to go pretty hard left on the next upwind, as he thought there was better pressure and good lifts on that side. We gained a ton of boats on this leg and rounded the windward mark in 12th, which is where we finished, as the last downwind was a parade, with very few position changes.

They jammed in a third race, as we had missed one on Monday, so we got one off first time this time. We were once again in good shape and moving well, but we had someone under our lee (Jim K in Doghouse, the boat retrieved from the bottom of the bay!) who forced us to tack away. We did a better job not tacking so much this leg, and used our boat speed to keep up with the fleet. However, we were trying to stay in the middle and boats on the left gained big. We again rounded in the bottom half. The wind was very slowly going light at this point, and the down winds were becoming as tactical as the up winds. We picked off a couple boats downwind again. We tended to take a more direct course, and everyone else was reaching higher and played luffing games, so we gained well.

The second windward was forgettable. We continued to lose places and rounded about fifth from the back. Steve reminded us that there was lots of racing left, because we had one more windward and leeward. We picked off a couple boats on the downwind, but the wind was down to 1 to 2 knots and the jibing angles were huge. As we were inching along, we spied a new breeze coming from the right shore, which was 10 miles away. Even though we were being headed, we hung onto the tack until we got into the breeze. We passed a bunch of boats on the reach into the finish and ended up 27th. We had a great sail home in freshening breeze, and the sun was setting.

So, our finishes for the day were 19th, 12th, and 27th, which put us 23rd after Day Two. However, the committee was going to allow us to count the first race the same as our average for the week, after throw-outs. So, if we could do well the next three days, we could count the first day's race higher than the 28th it was listed now. If we counted the first day's race under this ruling, we would jump from 23rd to the mid-teens, which was pretty good in this company. There were also a slew of protests that had to be heard, so other positions could've changed. If we could figure out a system for better starts, we could easily move up. All the top guys had bad finishes, including a 33rd by the great Brad Read. It was a tough day for the leaderboard, so we didn't feel so bad. We had beaten several of the top guys.

Wednesday, January 10

Wednesday was warmer and with even lighter winds than the day before – much like a Dillon day in late summer, when the winds can go light and very fluky. We were one of the last boats to get to the start, as Mark Laura had given us some pointers on how to get a little more speed and better pointing. We moved the mast butt back about 3/8", which made us feel better, but we were not really sure that it made a difference.

The first race got off in about 5 knots of breeze. We were doing well, probably in the top 12, when it was called due to the wind doing a huge shift. Ditto the second race, although we were not quite so far up in the standings. We were still having problems getting off the line in clear air with speed. We seemed to get sucked into other boats, who would gas us and force us to make extra tacks in bad air, which was killing us on the first leg.

We finally got in a whole race around noon. The wind had mostly clocked left, and we bet that it would continue to do so. We started pin end on starboard, but flopped to port right away, which was heavily favored. We were forced to tack back as a starboard tacker pushed us over, and we probably held on too long going to the left. When we tacked, we were almost laying the mark and we seemed to be in fresher breeze on the left. But when got up to the mark, we were mid pack again. They changed course downwind, and again it seemed like the fleet ignored it and stayed too high. We went low and jibed down the middle, keeping good speed and taking a more direct route, as the wind was slowly dying again. We picked up a bunch of boats and were probably in the top 15.

The leeward mark was a good one for us as we jibed from port to starboard, doused the chute, and set the genny in one smooth motion. Bob was really good on the foredeck and kept everything together. We held onto starboard for just a minute and then tacked for new breeze we saw coming from the far shore. Several boats went further left and right, and wasted distance. We were side by side with Chris Snow, and had delusions of grandeur as the wind got to us first, imagining we could beat him to the mark. The wind had gone right, which was more square, and we finished tacking to the windward mark in 13th, with lots of room around us.

The final run/reach was another tight one, as the wind was coming down in streaks and the direction was changing subtly with each. We first lost to Snow, then caught up at the end of the leg as we hung right a little longer, because we spied another new wind line coming from the ocean side. We quickly caught up with Snow, but were unable to pass him. We had our genny up and thought about throwing our chute to try to get by, but we decided not to until he did. And by then, of course, it was too late. We finished 13th, our second finish in the top 15.

It was so much like Dillon that it was funny. We were obviously in a transition zone between the prevailing winds, which were westerly, and the sea breeze, which was easterly. They fought each other all day and created havoc on the course. This race took so long that many of the boats didn't finish and were scored the same as the last boat to finish, which is 19th. What a dumb rule. We sailed a good race and only gained six points on the worst boat on the course!

The next race was started in a totally new breeze from the south, which petered out and then shifted west again, so they abandoned. Which was too bad, as we probably had our best start of the week so far. We were well away from the crowd with lots of speed, clear air, and no one to screw with us.

The sea breeze finally seemed to win, and came in from the east at about 5 knots. Steve said it would continue to oscillate to the right a bit, so he called for the committee boat end on starboard. We were right there, but we took an extra turn with 30 seconds to go, which left us moving too slowly to close out a boat who sneaked in at the last second. We convinced him to tack to port, which was a dumb idea because when we did the same, we were eating his bad air for a long time, and our boat speed was horrible. We went the right way though; as he rounded about 6th, we about 25th.

We rounded the weather mark, and again went down the middle as a lot of the fleet went way to the left. Not only did we have better breeze, but we were able to go more directly to the mark and we picked up a bunch of boats. When we rounded, we had a boat directly in front and slightly outside, and another behind and inside. We got in a shouting match with both. Peter bailed out to the inside of the mark rather than go outside the boat in front, who was screaming we had no room. We had to do a 360° penalty turn, which totally screwed up our chute and tangled it with the genny. So, we ended up having to spend some time trying to unravel that mess instead of going fast. We went from mid-20s to the back of the pack.

The next windward leg was uneventful, although we were picking the shifts well and we passed several boats. The next downwind was also dull. The last windward leg, we were once again mixing it up with some of the better boats at the finish. The same boat we had tangled with earlier just happened to be coming in on port and we on starboard. We couldn't make the line either, but we forced him over. Peter thought we could shut him out at the mark, but the guy did a good job of poking up inside us, and beat us by a hair. We ended up 32nd. Points so far put us 25th, but if we do the math for the first race we were 20th, with four races to go and one throw-out. We obviously had the ability to finish better, but weren't consistent.

Thursday, January 11

No wind today at all. We motored out to the middle of the ocean, it seemed like, and bobbed around for two hours before they called it. Peter was a believer in the minimalist approach, so we didn't have enough gas to get all the way back (again) and had to bum some off another boat. It took us almost two hours to get back. We then filled up our can and theirs. We went to Miami Beach and hung out for several hours people watching, and had dinner at a sushi place. Five white guys in a pimp mobile Cadillac – we were quite a sight! A good time was had by all.

Friday, January 12

The last day, unfortunately. We got lucky with the weather, though, as another cold front was pushing through and brought new wind with it. The temperature was in the low 70s. We had a much shorter motor, because the wind was coming from the south up the bay and appeared to be pretty steady at 3 to 5 knots. We were anxious to do better and set up to start well away from the rest of the fleet, toward the pin end. Steve and I thought there would be better wind on the left, although all the fast guys saw something on the right because they were all at the boat end.

We flopped to port soon after the gun, with almost no one around us. The wind slowly clocked to the left until we were pointing straight at the mark! It went back and forth a couple of times, but the trend was definitely lefty and we looked golden. There was one boat inside us that also did well and beat us to the mark, and a couple others that were way on the other side who found something over there. But we rounded 5th – our best rounding by far. We were ahead of all the fast guys.

We hung onto starboard jibe for a while, with the whole fleet in a parade behind us. We decided to jibe when enough of them also went to make sense for us to cover. Steve thought there was better breeze down the middle, even though it was chopped up from the boats still rounding. We managed to keep our position, as Luther and Peter were very good at keeping the boat moving in the light winds. We rounded 4th. We took the right gate mark, and hung onto starboard going back upwind for a while to clear our air from behind the chutes.

When we tacked we were in good shape, and once again saw nice lifts and better breeze on the left. We rounded in 4th again, but Mookie (Terry Hutchinson's boat) caught up to us and was breathing down our neck. They were trying to win the regatta, so were pressing pretty hard. We crossed some jibes with them, but they pulled a nice move right at the end to get up and over the top of us, and inside at the finish. We were still very pleased with a 5th. We beat all the top boats but Mookie and Siesta, the Japanese boat.

We figured that if clear air and speed worked once, it was probably good a second time. So, we hung out at the pin end again, but this time much closer to it, because this time we had company. We about had to tie Peter up to go for the line early enough, but we hit it with speed and only a touch late. Once again, the wind slowly began to shift left, but it was more persistent and not oscillating as much as the first race. We again ended up pointing right at the mark, with just a boat called War Party inside and ahead of us. They had not been really competitive over the week, so we were surprised to see them. None of the boats on the right did as well and we rounded second, with actually a pretty big gap behind, considering the number of boats on the course.

We followed War Party for a bit, and jibed inside when Steve again felt the pressure was better down the middle. We slowly but surely rolled over them, as Luther and Peter did their thing with the chute up. While War Party was watching the chute and trying to keep it full, we were steering the boat with our weight, with Luther subtly pumping the chute. (Repeated pumping was illegal.) We ended up rounding a good 3 or 4 boat lengths ahead, having started the leg several boat lengths behind.

We hung onto starboard for a bit, and tacked to port once we cleared the chutes rounding behind us. We were in a good controlling position on the fleet, going back to the middle of the course. We used a little of our lead to keep it and stayed between the fleet and the mark, and rounded still several boat lengths ahead. Salsa was now behind us. We didn't realize till too late that they were one of the top pro boats; they ended up 3rd for the regatta. They had been very slowly reeling us in after being 3rd at the first windward mark. Steve called for a jibe set and we went to the middle, looking for better wind. Fortunately we found it because Salsa held to the other side, and we split with them. We pretty much stayed away from them for the whole leg, and were just trying to find wind and stay moving.

This time, we picked the left mark and went back to windward on port, but on the right side of the course this time. We again let Salsa split with us, which made me nervous, but Steve was convinced that the right was favored. It was, but we had two bad tacks when Bob got the topping lift on top of the jib sheet and Luther couldn't tack all the way. Not ideal when you're in a dog fight!

We crossed Salsa once on starboard. As we neared the finish, they had caught up to within 2 boat lengths. At the last cross, we should have tacked to cover, but Peter insisted on one tacking to the finish. We'd be on port going for the pin end and Salsa would be on starboard, going for the boat end. They got the slightest of lifts and they beat us by a couple of boat lengths. It was disappointing to lead for so long and then lose it on the very last tack. We couldn't be disappointed with a 5-2 for the day, however, and with the averaging for Monday's race, we moved all the way up to 11th for the regatta. We were the third amateur boat – a great finish for us!

We hauled butt for the hoist, but some of the other guys kept their chutes up and beat us in. We weren't really ready, anyhow, as the car wasn't at the ramp; Bob had to bum a ride back to the other marina to get it. He showed up literally as we were pulling the boat from the water. The other guys took showers, and we headed over for dinner and the awards ceremony. They gave us best finish for Friday, which really wasn't correct as Salsa had 6-3/4 points to our 7 points, but Peter kept the beautiful trophy anyhow.

We stayed and drank for a while. I got a chance to talk to Terry Hutchinson, now the president of the America's cup syndicate, American Magic, and the winner of too many Championships to list, as well as the Rolex Yachtsman of the Year twice. He was gracious and friendly, and had won the regatta against some seriously tough sailors.

We finished one place behind Frank K and Mark Laura in 10th, and ahead of Jim K in 15th. He actually had a good last day and would have done much better, if he hadn't sunk. We beat one pro boat – no less than Jeff Johnstone, president of J boats and son of the founder, Bob Johnstone.

Saturday, January 13

Peter took Steve to the airport, then picked me up and we hung out for a while. Peter had left his outboard on the dock, but luckily some honest soul picked it up and was keeping it for him. Peter took Luther and me to the airport about 1:30, and he went to get the boat for the long drive home. The flight home was uneventful, except we got in a little late to Detroit and our bags didn't make it. It was good to see the family.

Conclusions

1) There was a small but significant gap between the top guys and the best amateurs. They have everything so wired, it was hard to find one area they have not covered to find a weakness. The boats were so optimized, and every detail has been examined and evaluated for the best, lightest, and strongest solution.

2) Even the great ones made mistakes in big fleets. All the top guys had a result of 15th or lower, and several had results in the 30s!

3) You can spend an enormous amount of money on a boat and still only be a top 15 contender. Jim K's boat was about as optimized as they get and he finished 15th, behind us. The amount of fine-tuning on the top boats was incredible. For instance, they have taken absolutely every block and line and made them as small and light as possible. The backstay tensioner line was 1/8", high strength stuff – same with the jib and main Cunningham lines. The turning blocks for all those adjustments were tiny dinghy blocks that looked far too small to carry any real load. The spinnaker winches had been removed to save weight, which was a real bear for the trimmer in big wind. They even snapped off the bolt heads that come through the toe rail on the inside of the cabin! They carried dehumidifiers to run after racing, so the boats wouldn't absorb humidity from the air. The top boats had new sails at every regatta, and there was definitely a difference there. Boat speed for the top guys was subtly but measurably better.

4) Starts were as important to big fleet racing as a big serve in tennis. You can win without a good start, but it's a hell of a lot more difficult. Getting off the line with speed and clear

air was critical – and getting the starts right was extremely difficult. Finding a space, much less being on the correct side of the course, judging the distance to the line, ensuring space to leeward, and hitting it with speed at the gun was a tricky business. We were not very consistent in this area. Peter tried to judge the line instead of trusting his crew, and we were consistently late and slow. However, we did a good job picking the correct end of the line and side of the course, which was Steve's call. If you got out in the top three or four boats, you had all the choices in the world. If you were back in the pack, you got knocked around and were unable to make the choices you wanted to follow your gameplan.

At Lake Dillon, even with only 15 boats on the starting line, the Committee boat end was usually the place where everyone wanted to be. But if you had a pack of boats all trying to win the right end of the line, only one or two were going to get away well. Everyone else would be eating bad air. I changed my starting strategy to coming in on port and flopping over to leeward of the pack of boats, getting clean air and going fast.

Until the last day, we were usually mixing it up with a number of other boats. I suggested my strategy to the team and when we tried it, and it mostly went well. I thought it better to start in the second row and do a clearing tack to get clear air, or to leeward, rather than try to find a hole on the line where you would probably get buried.

5) It was very difficult to learn from the top guys when you were back in the fleet. Not only did we not have the chance to see what they were doing, we couldn't tell what was really creating their advantage. When we were straight-lining with one of them and they were beating us, it could have been one of a hundred things; it may just have been that they had brand-new sails. While they tended to make fewer tactical, strategic, and sail-handling mistakes, they did make mistakes, and they were easier to see when made.

6) The depth of talent in the regatta was very impressive. Besides the professional guys already mentioned, there were a bunch of ex-college team sailors and other pros who were somehow in the business (like making boat parts). Many of these guys traveled to races all the time and sailed many different classes, so their depth of experience was much greater than we were typically exposed to. Our idea of a full season was three or four months on Lake Dillon, and a couple extra regattas. The J-24 class was carting all over the map to regattas. We had teams from Venezuela, Japan, Ireland, Italy, and Canada. It is truly an international game.

7) The J-24 was really a young man's boat. While you can steer or do tactician without much strain, it's uncomfortable for everyone but the skipper. I can't imagine a top boat having anyone much older than me (38 at the time) in any spot besides helm or tactician. (None of the top five did at this regatta.) The trimmer took a physical beating; the foredeck needed to be agile, light, and cat-quick; and the middle guys needed to wear armor because they took such a pounding from the boat, having nowhere comfortable to sit.

8) This is an expensive game if you want to compete at the top. It's possible to find a good boat for less than $10,000, but the amount of work a boat like that would take would run up to $15,000 to $17,000 pretty quickly. A boat that's $15,000 but ready to race is probably a smarter way to get started. (Remember, this was 1996!) Then, it takes a lot of money to stay competitive. The bottoms must remain perfectly smooth and to do that, they really need to be dry sailed – a difficult thing at Lake Dillon. The sails need to be replaced every two seasons or so, or they begin to look ragged.

9) You've got to have four people who know what they're doing, and a fifth for the extra weight. The proposed rule that would limit the weight to four people is a good one, I think, and would definitely have encouraged me to get into the class sooner. I have enough trouble trying to find three crew for

my boat. Having five every weekend adds that much more complexity to it.

This was an amazing experience – one I would try to recreate several more times over the next few years. Besides the usual sailing camaraderie, the exposure to some of the best sailors and programs in the country was a lot of fun. The J-24 is hardly Gran Prix sailing, but the level of professionalism and attention to detail is no less impressive. The regattas were very professionally run, with big sponsors and budgets. As an amateur, there were no delusions of grandeur. The professionals were bound to be on the podium spots. However, being able to race side by side with them was (and is) pretty unique to our sport.

Chapter Six

Doghouse and ChuckWagon

After I finished racing with the guys at Lake Dillon, I decided I wanted to do more bigger regattas. My first was the J-24 North Americans in Cleveland, racing for Jim K. His boat, Doghouse, had a funny graphic of a sad-looking dog in a doghouse, presumably a metaphor for many sailors and their plight at home.

Before I bought my Santana, I sailed with Jim's younger brother on his J-24. His boat was named Do Not Play On or Around This Dumpster, or Dumpster for short. His sailing buddies used to fill his cockpit with their empty beer cans after a day's racing. There was also a third brother, Tom, who sailed the Ensign. All were really good sailors. Frank won the Santana 20 Nationals held during the '24 Dillon Open.

Jim invited me to the J-24 North Americans in Cleveland. Unlike the Midwinters in Miami nine months earlier on ChuckWagon, we towed the boat across the country from Denver. Jim had a huge dually pickup truck with a giant 454ci V8. While most guys slow down to get better gas mileage, Jim was happy to hammer along at 80 MPH and 5 MPG. We uncomfortably slept in the bed of the truck or the back seat and drove straight through.

When we arrived in Cleveland, the weather was warm and sunny. Any cross-country trip first requires a visit to the pressure car wash to get all the bugs and road grime off. Jim had found us a nice hotel close to the venue, and we headed to the bar under threatening skies. The next day dawned rainy and gray, and the lake looked angry. Also like Miami, the water was a mess of steep waves created by the shallow shelf close to the shore. Jim brought his girlfriend/new wife (we weren't sure which) and she was not looking happy. However, she was a trooper all day and stuck with it, and us. I was to be trimmer for this regatta, a position I was very familiar with on other boats, but not the J-24. (At least I hadn't filled that role for a while.) The genoa is a handful and you needed good technique, not lots of muscle, to get it in. It needed to be sheeted about 90% of the way in by the end of the tack or you would end up doing a lot of grinding, which is both tiring and slow. Fortunately, the wind was in the low 20s, so it was blade jib weather, which that made it a lot easier.

While Miami had steep, short waves, these waves were something else altogether. Miami's waves were fairly small, not having a chance to build much in the mostly protected waters of Biscayne Bay. Cleveland's waves came from across the approximately 50-mile width of Lake Erie, then climbed the coastal shelf. By the time they got to our racecourse, they were both large and steep. And when I say steep, they were like falling off a cliff. You'd climb up the front, which was relatively gentle, then fall off the back, crashing into the water on the back side. It was about as uncomfortable as I've ever been on a sailboat. It was brutal. Jim was not anxious to experience a repeat of the sinking of Doghouse in Miami. So, after one wild broach with the spinnaker, we stuck to the jib down wind. Conditions were deteriorating. The Race Committee pulled the plug pretty early.

None of us, except perhaps Jim, were disappointed by this. So, we headed to the bar. The next day dawned even worse, with winds on the racecourse reportedly over 30 knots – too much for J-24s. They are small boats with small, not terribly efficient keels, and they get knocked around pretty hard in winds over about 25 knots. The sea state was a mess as well, with continued heavy chop. No one was too excited about going out. As it turned out, the first day's racing would end up being all we got, as the next was rained out as well. We ended up 25th out of 35 boats, and didn't break anything or anyone. Jim was incredibly kind and generous, and a good guy to travel with.

I raced with Peter and Chuck on ChuckWagon at the Midwinters the season before and liked them both. They were co-owners of the boat, which was not a common arrangement. In 1999, I committed to sailing with them on their J-24 in the Texas Circuit, finishing with the North Americans in Chicago later in the year.

* * *

I offered to help Peter tow the boat to Texas. The giant Cadillac had died on the drive home from Miami and had been replaced with an even bigger '70s Chevy Suburban with the venerable 454 V8 engine. As seemed fitting, we left in a driving May snowstorm. The first few hours were white knucklers, with heavy, wet snow blowing sideways across the highway, and I wondered about the wisdom of our timing. By midnight, we were through the worst of it and approaching Oklahoma. It was cold and dark, but there was no more precipitation. We got to our destination with no further drama.

The Texas Circuit was a J-24-only suite of regattas on some of Texas' best lakes, of which they have many. For us Colorado guys, who really have very few reasonable pieces of water, this was a mecca of large lakes, beautiful lakefront homes, and spectacular yacht clubs. These regattas also tended to be extremely well run, with good breezes, warm temperatures, and amazing hospitality. Some sort of incredible barbeque was usually the centerpiece of the events on shore, and we were frequently hosted by local J-24 owners in their huge homes. These regattas equaled the best-run regattas on the coasts that I had attended.

The sailors were also topflight, with some of the best J-24 boats in the country on the Circuit. Having consistently great competition to test against week after week honed their skills to a high shine. They were good – really good.

I had actually done a Texas Circuit regatta on Blue Side Down in the ---------------80s. We towed the boat down with an International Harvester Scout II, with a wheezy 345ci V8 engine that could barely get out of its own way. And having a short wheelbase, we were limited to about 60 MPH or the trailer would start pushing the tow car around. It was scary. We finished 7th out of 42 boats and actually won one race. The winner was no less than Paul Foerster, who went on to win three Olympic and two Pan American Medals. It was an amazing experience.

Back to 1999. We did three regattas – Lake Ray Hubbard near Dallas, Austin Yacht Club on Lake Travis, and Eagle Mountain Lake near Fort Worth. Fort Worth held a regatta with the quaint name of the Cowtown Stampede on Eagle Mountain Lake, northwest of the city. At over 8,000 acres, it is a big stretch of water (at least compared to Colorado!), with beautiful homes dotting its shores. The Fort Worth Boat Club was the host and they did a great job, with amazing food and parties and a well-run race series. The competition as per usual, was excellent, with 22 well-prepared and sailed boats in attendance.

Going into the last day of racing, we were well up in the standings, only needing a couple of solid races to win or place. This was rarified air for a Colorado boat, since we rarely were in the podium places at these regattas.

The normally consistent and reliable Texas breeze abandoned us this day, and we were treated to fluky and inconsistent winds. In our first race, we picked badly and ended up in 8th. This meant we had to finish in the top three in the last race to win the regatta. Our confidence was not very high. The last race started under gloomy skies, with winds of about 5 knots. The wind was shifty and there were some pretty good holes in it. We struggled to find clear wind and were well down in the teens as we approached the last leeward mark rounding. Spinnakers were limp and everyone was crawling toward the mark. Carefully, the mark was rounded and genoas gently sheeted in. Bouncing around on these boats in light wind completely unsettles them, and it's very slow.

When we rounded, Chuck suggested we take a flyer and hang onto a port tack, taking us at right angles to the next mark. We all thought he was crazy, but his logic was that if we couldn't make a big move we'd be off the podium altogether, so why not risk it? I am sure the rest of the fleet felt the same way: "What are those guys doing?!" As we crawled slowly away from the fleet, essentially going away from the finish line, the wind got even lighter and eventually just stopped. We were now probably a third of a mile from the racecourse. As we sat there bobbing up and down, Chuck whispered, "Look," and pointed in front of us. Sure enough, there was a new line of breeze peeking over the far shore, coming to the fleet on its starboard side.

I am sure the rest of the fleet was now looking on in horror as the new breeze reached us first. We slowly rolled onto a starboard tack and started moving. We only had the breeze to ourselves for a few minutes, because it filled in across the course soon enough. But it was enough to carry us from about 17th to 3rd and tied us for the regatta win. We sailed around almost every other boat as they sat helplessly watching. The Race Committee (RC) should probably have canceled the race, but it was Sunday afternoon and they wanted to get a last race in. This annoyed the local guys to no end, and there was a lot of grumbling on the dock afterwards. It was a brilliant roll of the dice by Chuck, and any of them could have done the same.

The tiebreaker was supposed to be who had the best score for the last day. By our math, that wasn't us, having been beaten by another boat by half a point. But to our surprise, the RC gave us the regatta win. (They had some logic for it, which I do not remember now.) We did not protest, as you can imagine! I think perhaps they were hoping more Colorado boats would come down for the races, as generally the more boats the better. As per usual, the Texas sailors were gracious in defeat and gave us a rousing round of applause when we were presented with the winner's trophies. The crew got trophies as well, and mine sits proudly in my office to this day.

J-24 NAS

Next stop was Chicago and the J-24 North Americans. Peter and I drove the boat pretty much straight through from Texas to Chicago. He had arranged for a place to leave it until we came back in July for the regatta. This was to be my fourth national regatta in a J-24. Like the others, this one was well organized and well attended with 45 boats, and had the usual group of rock stars, including Geoff Moore, a former National Champion. Most of the top boats had at least one professional on board, and the competition was fierce. Like other big regattas with a lot of boats, getting off the line with clear air was king. Being in the perfect place on the line, or right on time, was less important than having clear air. Moore ended up winning the nine-race regatta, actually only winning two races, and with a worst race of 26th. Of the nine races, there were seven different winning boats! We finished 10th, the third best amateur boat. We had three finishes of 7th or better, a number in the teens, and one 41st.

Conditions on the first day were amazing – hot temperatures with consistent winds around 10 knots. With a lack of big shifts, boats spread out left and right, banging corners to minimize tacks. There were times when the boats on either side were over a mile apart, so it was very difficult to judge where you were, until you got to the marks and started counting boats. On the first day, we had results of 13th, 7th, and 12th, which we were very pleased with. We obviously had good boat speed and were making good decisions to keep our air clean. We'd learned a lot from the Midwinters in Miami in '96.

It was a blast to be on a line with 44 other boats. Credit to the Race Committee for keeping us more or less under control. There were a number of general recalls, when large groups of boats went over early. After a couple of those, the RC "black flagged" the start, meaning if you were over early, you were disqualified. The top guys assumed that if everyone was over, they would be protected by a general recall. So, they were super aggressive at the starts, knowing they needed a good one to get in the top 10 and have a chance to win the regatta.

Day Two dawned the same, and we picked up where we left off. The day's results were 17th, 15th, and finishing the day with a 3rd, our best result of the weekend. The next day the wind went away, and we motored out to sit for a couple of hours before the RC called it. While waiting, we went swimming in the amazingly clear water off the city of Chicago. Chicago had a reputation of having gross water in the Chicago River and along the city shoreline, but that was not our experience. They introduced zebra mussels that transformed the water from a murky sludge near the shore to crystal clear just a mile offshore. You could easily see 10' to 20' into the water, and it was beautifully warm as well. We were a bit sad to give up on the swimming, but the bar was calling.

The last racing day came, with fresh and steady winds. We started the day with a terrible 41st, but finished strong with a 15th and another 3rd, leaving us tied for 10th overall. However, we lost the tie breaker. We were the third boat without a professional on board. With no throw-outs due to the missed racing day, the 41st really hurt us. If that had been a race finish in the teens, we would have finished 7th overall. Not bad for weekend warriors from Colorado!

Peter had arranged for us to stay at a friend's apartment near the yacht club. There were two problems, though: they didn't have beds for all of us and it wasn't air conditioned. So, we slept on the floor and sweated through hot summer nights in Chicago.

We drove the boat home to Colorado after the regatta. I volunteered to take the first shift, as we exited the city. This was hairy enough, as a J-24 sits very high on its trailer with a 3' keel, plus it's a full 8' wide. Navigating the narrow Chicago city streets was not fun. At one point, I was approaching a narrow bridge that also felt too low for us to get under. At the same time, a fire truck was coming up behind with lights and sirens blasting, trying to move people out of the way. As I drew closer to the bridge I heard like the voice of God, someone call out over a loudspeaker: "Hey, you and the boat, get that thing out of the way!" It wasn't like I was TRYING to be in the way! I pulled over at the next possible opportunity, with my nerves pretty well shot. Fortunately, the rest of the drive home was uneventful.

Chapter Seven
The Judge

The next summer, I had no boat. So, I connected with Dave H, the current owner of Blue Side Down, the boat I had started racing on in Colorado 17 years earlier. Dave was an excellent sailor and the boat was a proven winner, so he had no shortage of people wanting to crew for him. However, I had beaten him in the overall the year before (by one place), so I had a bit of credibility. My excellent foredeck, Craig, was also looking for a new boat, so we came aboard as a duo, in addition to his trimmer and tactician, Luther T. Yes, the same Luther I had done the J-24 Midwinters with a few months earlier. Luther was a bit of a legend on Lake Dillon. He'd sailed there for MANY years and had a sixth sense about the lake and its fluky, unpredictable winds.

Since there were quite a few boats for every race, the Race Committee typically ran us on circle routes, which included reaching legs. This kept boats from being in each other's way, but it was not the typical windward/leeward kind of racecourses that bigger regattas set. These courses would take us to the corners of the lake, frequently making for tricky winds. Knowing which way new breeze would arrive, and at what strength, was a real advantage, so Luther was a key to Blue Side Down's success over the years. Dave was always at the top of both the J-24 fleet and the PHRF overall.

Craig was simply one of the best foredecks on the lake, and he fit right in with Dave and Luther. I was the sewer position, which meant I was basically in charge of getting the spinnaker ready to set, and make sure it didn't come out in a tangle. I spent a lot of time below with piles of sail cloth around me. I also was "rail meat" or adding weight on the side deck to help balance the boat. Like most racing keelboats, the crew is expected to hike out as far as they legally can. This makes a huge difference, especially on a boat like the J-24, with a small keel.

Going upwind, I was expected to get from one side of the boat to the other without getting in anyone's way. Craig went around the front of the mast, and Luther and Dave took up most of the cockpit. Luther had to bring the large overlapping genoa from one side to the other and was all elbows while doing it. I had to slide under the boom on my back as described earlier.

The crack crew combined with a fast boat ensured another victory for Blue Side Down and Judge Helmer. We won both the J-24 fleet (25 boats) and PHRF Overall (58 boats) for the Summer Series, as well as the J-24 fleet in the Dillon Open (28 boats). It was about as dominant a summer campaign as there could be. It was as much fun as I'd had racing, working with three top-notch guys, sailing at a consistently high level, and really dominating. Dave was a generous and mostly pleasant guy to sail for. He was not a yeller, but could get excited when things got frantic. He never abused the crew and was always happy to buy a beer later. I saw Dave in 2023 at the Dillon Open and he was still as ebullient as ever. Blue Side Down was now being loaned to a young woman for racing and was a bit worse for wear, but it was great to see the old girl.

Chapter Eight

Psycho Duck

After spending several seasons on J-24s, I became interested in the Santana 20. While it sounds like it should be similar to the 22 I used to own, they were completely different boats. The S-20's total weight was about the same as the keel on my old 22! It was sailed with three crew max: the helm, who also handled the main sail controls, a trimmer, and foredeck.

John and Steve were brothers who owned an S-20 together as a brotherly activity. John was overweight and had to be the helm because he couldn't move well enough to fill either of the other positions. The problem was, he didn't have a lot of experience or a good feel for the helm. Steve was tall and strong, and well suited for the foredeck, since it was a job best done standing on the cabin floor just aft of the mast. If you were tall and had long arms, you could get the pole on and off the mast and handle the jib and genoa without going forward of the mast or getting out of the cabin opening.

At this point, I had a ton of J-24 experience and had helmed my own boat pretty successfully. I liked both brothers, and agreed to come on board to see if we could improve their results. The S-20 fleet was and is pretty active in Colorado. It's an easy boat to tow and rig, and only needs three crew. So, it made it easier to find crew than a J-24, which must have four and sometimes five. And like the J-24, it rewards constant sail adjustments and proper crew weight placement. Being 20' and lighter, it was also a lot cheaper to campaign. Plus, not being as popular as the J-24, there weren't as many professionals in the fleet, allowing a better chance for weekend warriors to compete at big regattas.

This was one of the most frustrating periods in my sailing and racing career. While the brothers claimed they wanted to improve and achieve better results, John was not suited to be on the helm. He struggled to get the boat in a groove up wind and tended to oversteer. Helming a small keelboat takes a light touch, and he didn't have one. Being the main trimmer and also in control of the backstay, he effectively controlled the accelerator.

Small keelboats heel over easily in puffs. Typically, the backstay is pulled on, the traveler let down, or the main sheet let out (or all three) to help keep the boat driving forward and not going sideways. Meanwhile, the helm also needs to steer the boat. It's a bit like patting your head and rubbing your tummy – it takes lot of multitasking to get right.

John did not move side to side in the boat on tacks or gybes very well, and was always getting tangled up with the tiller, mainsheet, or both. On a boat as small and light as the S-20, this was slow, and our results reflected it. We struggled through most of our regattas, making dumb mistakes and/or just being consistently slow.

We had one decent regatta, at Alcova Reservoir in central Wyoming. This stunning lake is an amazing place to sail. At about 2,500 acres, it's large enough to allow for lots of other water activities and not feel cramped. Santana held their S-20 North American Championship there in 1999, so we loaded up Steve's RV and towed the boat to Wyoming. There's an active sailing fleet (Casper Boat Club) at Alcova, and a nice clubhouse with good camping. We stayed in Steve's RV, and there was a good party Saturday night. There were 32 boats from all over the country.

We finished 5th out of 32 boats, which was by far the best result we'd ever had. Winds were typical of the high plains, fluky and uneven. This suited me, having had so much experience on Lake Dillon. Our boat handling was better than usual, and John kept us moving better than usual as well.

Our S-20 had the mainsheet roughly two-thirds of the way back in the cockpit, and had a small stainless steel plate of about 4"x4"that stuck out forward in my direction. Generally, John stayed behind the traveler and I was in front of it. When he hiked out, he could move his weight forward and use the plate to brace his foot. Being at least 250 pounds, having his weight outboard and forward when we were heeling over was very important. I was around 175 pounds and Steve only just over 200 pounds. We were on John constantly to move forward and out to help keep the stern out of the water – one of the many reasons we tended to be slower than other boats.

A few weeks later, we were racing a weekend regatta at Cherry Creek Reservoir. It was fall and the winds were stronger (and flukier) than the middle of summer, when there could be no wind at all. We were back to old habits, going slowly and making bad decisions, with rough boat handling. Steve and I were trying to anticipate gusts and doing a good job of communicating to John what we thought was coming, but he just wasn't getting it. He was really struggling to keep the boat in a groove with the fluky winds, and we had a couple of auto tacks when a new gust came in at an odd angle. This would slam the boat over with the genoa backed, creating a mess in the boat. We frequently would end up sailing the wrong direction after one of these auto tacks.

Toward the end of the day, we were getting angry all around. We had another auto tack, during which I fell very hard against the little stainless-steel plate on the traveler. It hit me just above the waistline in the middle of my back and hurt like a son of a bitch. I ended up with a large bruise and a painful back for days.

After the terrible day of sailing, hitting this plate and hurting myself was the last straw, and I lost my temper with John. I also resolved in that instant that I was no longer sailing with them on Psycho Duck. It had been two long frustrating seasons and we were not making any progress. It was clear that as long as John was on the helm, we were going to be mid or back of the fleet. Obviously, I couldn't ask them to split up, since the boat was their shared activity. I needed to go.

When we got back to the dock, and had a chance to settle down and crack a beer, I didn't feel any differently, and told them I was out. This was on the Saturday of a two-day event, so I was probably going to leave them without a crew for the Sunday races. We were also planning to do another regatta in a couple more weeks at another lake, and I said I wouldn't be doing that either. I was done for good. I know it was a shock to them both, but they seemed to understand. I felt like I had done all I could. The point was to try and get better, and that wasn't happening with the people we had.

Perhaps I was too rash and not patient enough. After all, I'd had a tiller in my hand from the age of four. I had a good feel for how a boat moves, when it's working, and when it isn't. John just didn't have that feel and wasn't learning it, as far as I could tell. I felt badly about leaving them in the lurch, and it was a bad way to end what had mostly been a good relationship all around.

* * *

When I got home, I received a scathing email from Steve, calling me all kinds of names and blaming me for everything. It was a horrible letter, probably the worst of its kind I ever received. I tried calling him right away, but his wife, said he didn't want to talk to me. I wrote back, trying to extend an olive branch, apologizing for the suddenness of my decision and sharing some of the thoughts behind it. But I didn't get a reply. We never spoke again, and I lost touch with both of them.

I am pretty sure the boat was sold out of state, as it popped up recently at the Dillon Open, with a yacht club in Oregon as home port. Or maybe it was just a coincidence that two S-20s were named Psycho Duck, but I doubt it. I have wondered a number of times what happened to the brothers and to the boat.

Chapter Nine

The O'Day and the Pelican (Lake, That Is)

In 2012, I was helping my dad put his boat in Aurora Reservoir, when I saw a little monohull sitting on gravel in the parking lot that had clearly been blown off its trailer. It said O'Day 19 on the side and looked to be a nice little boat. There was a large cockpit and a small two-berth cabin. Amazingly, the sails were still both on her, as well as a trolling motor on the stern! I was shocked someone hadn't used their five-finger discount to steal that, as it would have come off in seconds.

I called the Aurora Park Service and asked if they would forward my name to the owner to see if they might be interested in selling her. Turns out this was the second time it had blown off. The first time, it took eight guys to get her back on the trailer. At 1,400 pounds, she was not very big, but not an easy load to move! Apparently, he hadn't learned his lesson or how to tie her down, as she came off again. The winds can be wicked in Aurora! We used to bury stakes in the ground and tie our boat to them to ensure it would not come off the trailer. Besides the scratches on the hull side, she looked to be in decent shape.

Well, he called me and said he wasn't really interested in selling her, but it was obvious he was not interested in owning her anymore either. So, I asked what he might want for her. He said $900, which I thought to be a pretty ballsy ask, given its current condition and situation. I said I would give him $500 for the boat and $50 for the trolling motor, which he immediately accepted. I knew I would need a crane to get her back on the trailer, which was going to cost at least

$250. The main sail was a mess, although the jib was decent. And it would take some time to fix the gravel scars on the hull's side.

After transferring the title and money, I had the challenge of getting the mast down. The mast pivoted on a large bolt at the base and could be let down gently with a winch. But the boat was on its side, so it was impossible to take the mast off in the normal manner. It was sticking wildly into the air at about a 45° angle. The trick was that the side stays and forestay needed to be removed without the mast falling. I thought I could just muscle it, since it was not a big mast. I was incorrect. I figured out a way to release the high side stay while holding the mast, but as soon as the load was released, the mast fell right out of my arms and crashed to the gravel. Fortunately, aluminum is both sturdy and flexible, and no damage was caused.

Once I removed the mast and boom, I arranged to have a crane come out. It was hilarious. They don't really make small cranes, so a huge 20-ton (40,000 pounds) behemoth came out to pick up my little 1,400-pound boat. I carefully helped place the straps, since I was pretty sure he had never lifted anything like it. Even though we were way under the crane's capacity, it was a nervous thing to pick her off the gravel and get her nestled on the trailer again. It didn't take more than about 30 minutes, but they charged for the trip out and back. Still, it was worth the $250. I don't think I have eight friends who could've helped put her back on the trailer.

* * *

Then, the repair and upgrade work started. The scratches were not terrible, but needed a lot of sanding and filler. At this point in my life, I didn't have a suitable place to work on the boat, so I had her in a storage facility – for free, it turned out. My dad's neighbor owned a golf cart dealership with a boat, trailer, and RV storage facility attached to it, so I got the "friends and family" discount.

At this time, I didn't have a lot of battery-powered tools, and power from my storage spot to the main building was too far to stretch an extension cord. So, I used my one battery-powered drill with a sanding disc until the battery died, and a small generator my dad owned. Turned out that it only lasted an hour with a tank of gas, so that wasn't much help either. It took a lot of back and forth to get it sanded down. Then, finding the right color proved to be impossible. The boat was decades old, so even if I could find the original color, it would never match the faded hull. I ended up with something close. I wasn't going to obsess over a $500 boat!

I ordered a new mainsail and kept the little 100% jib. The new main was ordered from a generic loft for $550. It ended up being quite a nice sail. The boat came with the oddest cleats/snubbers for the jib. They were about the size of the smallest winch made, with a notch down the middle made of wood. I think the theory was that you would take a loop around the base, then pull the tail through the slot to keep it from slipping. They looked terrible and not like they would work, so I asked for some tiny winches (#5s) for Xmas, which Santa provided. That turned out to be a perfect upgrade. I also added cam cleats to properly and easily cleat the sail. She was starting to look like a sailboat again.

The small cabin had a couple of pretty nice orange cushions for the V berth and reasonable room for a cozy couple. No head or sink, though; it reminded me of the Maraudeur we had when I was a kid!

* * *

My thought for the boat was to take her to Minnesota. My then fiancée's family had a cottage on a pretty lake called Pelican Lake. The cottage was a small three-bedroom, one-bath house with no insulation of any kind. Also no ceiling, which meant listening to snoring every night. It could also get really hot during the day, even with a window A/C unit. One curiosity was that although there was a shower head, it didn't work. And the property was on a septic system, so conserving water was a must.

Many of the lakeshore properties had been upgraded with grand homes, including the neighbor to the north. But lots of the original cottages remained, so it was an incongruous mix of old (small) and new (large). The neighbor had a newer Catalina 22, a lovely little boat for the lake. Of course, I showed interest and we had a sail on her as well. He was not an experienced sailor and appreciated getting some tips.

When we were there, I missed having a shower, so came up with an idea that got me in trouble. The sun shone most days, so I would lay a solar shower bag in the grass to heat up during the day. I could then lift the heated shower bag to a large horizontal tree branch using a pulley, tossed over the branch with a hammer on a rope. I could have a nice hot shower, albeit in my swimsuit. Apparently, this annoyed the Catalina 22 neighbor and he complained to my fiancée's parents. I thought this was incredibly petty and given our shared sailing interest, didn't think he would have made a fuss. Obviously, I was wrong. The solar showers ceased.

Lake Pelican was about 5 miles long and 1-½ miles wide. The wind was mostly very nice and steady, except when a bad storm came through. The cottage had a boat dock and a lift for a small power boat they kept there. There really wasn't enough room to keep my sailboat on the dock, and I was nervous about what would happen if the wind came up, so I made plans to create a mooring in the relatively sandy shallow water just offshore. I couldn't sink a huge concrete block, which is the normal way to anchor a mooring, because A, I didn't have one (nor the capability of getting it in the water) and B, I didn't want to go to that much work and expense.

* * *

Towing the boat from Pelican Lake from Denver was uneventful, but I found out how important a good tow car is. We had a Subaru Outback with the base engine and a CVT (Continuously Variable Transmission). Without going into the details of how a CVT works, it basically means there are no gears: the transmission can find any number of gear ratios based on the terrain and the load. The car was tow rated at 2,700 pounds, which seemed to be plenty, even though we were traveling with three people, luggage for 10 days, the boat, and the trailer.

The engine and tranny seemed to handle the load OK, but the transmission was constantly trying to find the best ratios. As we would go up the slightest incline, the engine RPM would start to go up, sometimes ending in a crescendo of noise and vibration. It was highly irritating, going up and down, up and down for over 1,000 miles. We got there, but it was not a trip I wanted to make again in that car!

I borrowed a couple of sand screws, intended for camping on beaches. They were about 3' long and had a single screw blade about 6" up from the bottom. So, most of the device was just a long shaft. My first thought was to set them in a line and moor in the middle between them. The idea was to split the load, but it was obvious that this would prevent the boat from swinging properly. So idea #2 was to place them a couple of feet apart, with two lines to a fender that would act as a float that I could pick up when returning from a sail.

The problem was that I had to get them screwed into the lakebed – without diving gear. I had to dive down 30 to 40 seconds at a time, get a couple of turns in, then come back to the surface for a breath. It took a LONG time going up and down repeatedly before I had them screwed into the lakebed. But I felt they were very secure and there would be no chance they could pull out. To get to the boat, I had to wade out from the shore in water up to about my chest, then climb a swim ladder. Fortunately, the water was pretty mild, although the temperature was always a shock.

The system worked well and I enjoyed several absolutely sparkling sails, both with the family and by myself. Temperatures were in the mid 80s, and the breeze mostly between 10 and 15 knots. The boat was pretty easy to single-hand, with a small jib and winches close at hand. The new main set perfectly. Sitting against the lifelines, with the tiller in one hand and the mainsheet in the other, was a lot of fun. It was some of the best sailing I have ever done, especially on my own. It took well over an hour to tack up the length of the lake, then a leisurely return, gybing back and forth on beautiful blue water and clear skies.

One night, a wicked storm came in and I was very worried about how the boat would survive. Winds were well into the 40s and 50s, and blowing onto shore. If my mooring system came loose, the boat would very quickly be on the rocky shore and bashed to bits. There wasn't much I could do but wait. The next morning, I was relieved to see the boat was right where I'd left it. I swam out and inspected the sand screws. One had pulled almost all the way out, while the other seemed still well fixed. The one that had pulled out had clearly unscrewed itself from the lakebed, as the mooring line was a twisted mess. I wondered about the physics of this and how it was possible.

I had also brought a couple of dog leash screws, which were designed to be screwed into the ground and a dog leash attached. They were about 15", with most of the length being the screw itself. So, I re-screwed in the long sand screw, placed the dog screw next to it, and lashed the two together. Then, I repeated the process on the other one. I thought this would prevent the sand screws from turning out of the lakebed – and I was right. We had another wicked storm a few nights later and when I checked the next morning, nothing had moved at all. The fact there were now four screws in the lakebed probably helped ensure that nothing was going to come loose. I was quite pleased with myself and my ingenuity!

We had a fun 10 days. Since we were not coming back that summer, I needed to pull out the boat and put it on the trailer to be left for next year. Reluctantly, I waded out for the last time, and started the trolling motor to run over to the boat ramp, which was about two miles away. When I got close to the boat ramp, I pulled on the line to raise the centerboard, and it came up in my hand. The line had separated from the centerboard itself, so I had no way to raise the board! Fortunately, the trailer was designed in such a way that the centerboard would fold up as the boat was loaded. I would have to figure out a way to re-attach a new line with the boat in the water at a later time. We parked the boat in a corner of the driveway, covered her with a large tarp, and left for the winter.

* * *

Unfortunately, I was never to sail that lovely little boat on Pelican Lake (Or anywhere else.) again, as I split up with the fiancée a few months later. She asked that I get the boat, as it was obviously still parked at her family's cottage. So, I borrowed my dad's Lexus RX350 and arranged for my adult son to come with me to pick her up. As usual, he was a great driving companion and we had a quick drive out, staying at a cheap motel in the closest town to the lake.

The next morning, we went out to the cottage to find the boat looking a bit battered. The tarp was still in place and obviously had had a ton of snow on her; one of the stanchions had pushed through the deck, breaking the fiberglass and the backing plate. It would have taken a huge amount of force to do this. The stanchion itself was not bent, which surprised me.

The hull was full of water from rain and snow getting through the hole, so I spent over an hour bailing her out with a bucket. I wished I had brought a pump! While I had planned ahead and brought a small compressor, anticipating that the tires would need inflating, we needed a power source and had no way to get into the garage. Fortunately, one of the side doors was open, so we went in, ran a power cord to the boat, and got her pumped up. Our trip back was uneventful, with my son playing games as to how much fuel efficiency he could get towing the boat. The Lexus was a far superior tow vehicle to the Subaru for such a light load. It was quiet and luxurious, and only struggled going up steep inclines.

I really had no reason to keep the boat without a place to sail her. I could have put her in somewhere in Colorado, and probably should have done that, but decided instead to sell her. But now, I had a new project – a big hole in the side deck where the stanchion had busted the hull. It was probably 4"x3" and against the outer rail, making it an awkward place to get to. My plan was to put a couple of longitudinal pieces of 1" box section aluminum tube underneath for strength, then bolt through the deck. I would put a fiberglass patch both on the deck and below for the stanchion to sit on. The new bolts would be visible on the deck, but I wanted to make sure it was plenty strong if someone fell against it.

All went well, although getting to the underside of the deck required contortionist work on my part in a locker. I had to lay down on my back with my feet sticking out into the cockpit and do all the work upside down. This was unpleasant enough, trying to get nuts on bolts and so forth. But it got REALLY messy when I had to apply epoxy to the fiberglass. I managed to avoid getting it in my face or eyes, but when I examined the final product, I am not sure how! It was not my cleanest work.

The other problem, of course, was that the centerboard no longer had its lifting line. It was not obvious how I was going to solve this problem. The golf cart facility where I was keeping the boat was actually an old rocket manufacturing facility (Martin Marietta, I believe), with a huge shop and a 50-ton crane. I asked my dad's neighbor if I could use it for a few hours, which he agreed. This crane was designed to move rockets around their warehouse/manufacturing facility and was absolutely gigantic.

Once again, my little boat was child's play for such a massive crane, and we quickly had her suspended and the centerboard down. It did make me nervous to have her hanging in the air several feet above the concrete floor of the workshop, with my son working underneath. We drilled a hole, installed a new stainless-steel shackle, and ran a new line to the cockpit. Quick and easy, as it turned out, especially with my son there to help with the work. He is a mechanical engineer and understands how things work, even if he's not a sailor.

I sold the O'Day to a guy from Pueblo for $2,000, with the new sail and hull patched, the centerboard line installed, and new winches and cleats fitted. He didn't want the trolling motor, which I sold on craigslist for $50. I thought it was a fair price and a decent return for all the work I put into her. I had created a much nicer boat from a neglected and forgotten wreck. My pleasant memories from those ten days on Lake Pelican are priceless! I hope she gave the next owner as much joy as she gave me.

Chapter Ten
Community Sailing of Colorado

I stopped sailing for quite a while after selling the O-Day 19. I wasn't really in touch with any of the racing programs anymore and had lost interest in owning my own boat. I was plenty busy with teenagers' activities.

Kathy and I worked for the same company when we met. She was 42 and I was 56. But we were in similar situations at that point in our lives, both in unhappy relationships and looking for something more. We very slowly fell in love, left our respective relationships, and decided to move in together. Both of our separations (husband for her, fiancé for me) were very messy, especially hers, as she had been married for 14 years. Kathy was not a sailor, another reason I lost interest.

In about 2018 we went to the "Boat Show" in Denver. I put the title in quotes as it has become a powerboat-only show. There were two sailing related booths – Community Sailing of Colorado and some guys showing beautifully built and maintained wooden boats. This is in stark contrast to the very active sailing community there was when I moved to CO in 1976. CSC as it turned out would get me back into sailing and excited once again.

CSC provides sailing exposure to underserved populations like inner city kids and paraplegic and quadriplegic patients at Craig Hospital. They also run summer sailing camps for kids of all ages, at both Cherry Creek and Boulder Reservoirs. They have a fleet of Optimists, RS Teras and Topaz dinghies for smaller kids as well as a few 420s and Lasers for the more advanced young sailors. To keep track of the kids on the water, they have a good-sized fleet of small power boats, mostly 13' Boston Whalers, which I was to become very familiar with.

I started talking to the folks there and found out they were always looking for volunteers, both on the water and helping fix all their boats. The Topaz's and Tera's are rotomolded plastic, so built of the same stuff as kayaks. This makes them incredibly durable and require very little repair. The other sailing boats and the Whalers are all fiberglass, meaning dings and dents need to be repaired, something I was pretty familiar with. Plus they needed experienced sailors to take people out sailing. They had open sailing nights where people interested in going sailing would sign up, and me and other volunteers would take them out for an hour or so. These evenings were a lot of fun as folks were always keen and excited to be on the water.

CSC also had a couple of 17' sailboats designed to allow for para and quadriplegic people to go sailing. They had forward facing chairs, not unlike a racing seat in a race car. We would winch the patient into the seat, then securely strap them in. Every patient also had a care giver, sometimes a nurse. The responsibility of taking these people sailing was pretty nerve racking. Obviously if the boat capsized, they had no way of helping themselves. We never had any kind of problem, and we followed strict safety protocols. The rewards were well worth it.

Many of these people had been active before some terrible accident so being able to get out of the hospital was a real joy for them. Many were also very nervous about being in an exposed situation they had little control of. We had one young quadriplegic woman on the boat who had never been sailing before and she was very scared. The evening was beautiful with temperatures in the low 80's and a lovely breeze. There was less powerboat traffic than normal so conditions were perfect. After a bit she calmed down and eventually closed her eyes. After about 20 minutes her caregiver asked her how she was doing and she opened her eyes and said: "Beautiful." It was perhaps the highlight of my sailing career.

* * *

As it turned out, I was to spend MANY more hours repairing boats for CSC than sailing. But it was work I was able and willing to do, and they really needed the help. My first big project was a 13' Whaler from the mid 70's. Most of the Whalers had a heavy cloth rub rail which helped protect the boat and anything it might bump into (Which happened frequently with mostly teenage drivers!) from damage. These were screwed into the top edge of the Whaler. The boat I received had the cloth rub rail removed, to expose hundreds of old screw holes, as well as four very large holes on each corner. These were one to two inches across and an inch deep. All the wood had been removed, and a replacement wood package had been ordered from Boston Whaler in Florida for the cost of $550!

I went around and counted all the holes and there were over 300! Most were on the rub rail, so I had many sessions of applying thickened epoxy followed by many, many hours of sanding. I also discovered underneath the floor of the boat at the stern was full of water. These boats were built of a sandwich of two pieces of fiberglass with about an inch of foam in between. If holes from the wood seats and consoles were not sealed properly, water would get into the foam and waterlog the boat. So I decided to fix it as best I could and cut out two large sections aft, then dug out the soaked foam and let it drain for about a week. The foam was not closed cell, meaning water under the rest of the floor would leak out. I tilted the boat up as high as I could and waited.

It took a week for the water to stop, and I sucked it up many times as it puddled. Once I was pretty sure it was as dry as possible, I used spray foam to fill the holes I'd made and cut a couple of pieces of ½" plywood to go over the foam I'd applied. I used a multitool with a small blade to shave the foam nice and flat. Then I applied one piece of fiberglass tape along the seam and another larger piece of glass over the whole wood section, overlapping the fiberglass floor, and epoxied it well. Lots more sanding later, I had a very solid and strong repair that stood up well over time.

Next up was to paint. Lots more sanding and prep work inside the boat led to a couple of coats of VERY smelly two-part primer and then

4 coats of white paint. Boat paint is incredible stuff. It dries extremely hard and leaves a shiny finish. But there are nasty chemicals in it, and they are incredibly stinky. They really need to be applied in an open space and left to dry. They don't like big variations in temperature as they cure, which is a problem in Colorado! After doing the inside of the boat it was time to flip it over and get to the bottom. I had a couple of the CSC folks come over and we flipped her over and put her bottom up, back on the trailer.

I used the same primer and paint on the top sides, the part of the hull between the water line and rub rail. Then I prepped the actual bottom and what else, more sanding! (And epoxy patching.) Then primer and an anti-fouling paint called VC-17. She was going to go back to the club like this, and they were going to install the Whaler wood kit.

It was a great project and I felt good about bringing the old girl back to life. She wasn't perfect by a long shot. The areas of non-skid were badly cracked and I made the decision to not sand it all flat, so there were plenty of little cracks in many parts of the boat. But the paint job held up well, and she provides good service to CSC. In the end I spent 56 hours of labor and about $440 in fiberglass, epoxy, paint, and other supplies. (Which came out of my pocket.)

In the years that followed there were several more Whaler projects. One was refinishing all the wood, which I did with varnish, a process I will not repeat on these boats. It looks beautiful, but takes a lot of time with multiple coats required and lots of sanding in between. It also requires regular ongoing maintenance, which is great if it's on your own boat. But these boats are maintained by guys like me – volunteers and so I would use another solution going forward.

Another project was a 17' Whaler of the same era (mid 70's) that had a full wood console with a glass wind shield. The boat was in excellent shape, and CSC decided to try and sell it to make a profit rather than subject it to the rugged conditions of the sailing club. They'd bought it for $3,000, and I was seeing examples going for up to $10,000 on the coasts, but mostly with more modern engines. It also had a mid-60's era 65HP Mercury straight six, two stroke engine, which would not have been suitable for the organization, even if we could get it working. It would suck gas, be very smelly and require a lot more maintenance than a more modern engine.

The original wood consoles, especially with the wood windshields, were incredibly rare as they did not last very well. Boston Whaler switched to more and more fiberglass for their consoles over the ensuing years to help with longevity.

The wind screen was split into 4 pieces – two that faced forward and two that faced port and starboard. They were all held in place with old gaskets and a wood frame. There was a proper bench seat behind the console and another in front of it. It was all done in mahogany and a couple of the support pieces that held the console up right and to the boat floor were rotted.

Some of the wood was in very poor shape with the outer skins of plywood close to or almost completely gone. Some of the wood was in pretty good shape, especially the solid pieces, and I could tell a good sanding and wood oil would bring her back to life. I was definitely not going to try and varnish all of this wood as it would not stand up very well, and require a ton more work on my part. I also needed to source some kind of wood that would replace the rotted supports. I found a piece of ¾" teak plywood in Florida that was close to the mahogany and would hold up well. The 2'x4' piece was $125! After several hours of removing screws, I had the wind screen and both benches off. I decided to leave the actual base of the console in place, which turned out to be a good idea. I already had a jigsaw puzzle of wood pieces I would need to put back together!

So the sanding started. Every piece needed decades of neglect removed, and it was a long and painstaking task. Once everything was rough sanded with 60 grit, I had to go back over it with a finer grit to leave a smoother finish. I patched some of the worst spots around the wind screen frame with epoxy. Then each piece was wiped with water and then again with acetone before the wood oil was applied. I cleaned the glass gaskets, which amazingly, came out quite well and didn't disintegrate. I also VERY carefully cleaned each glass piece (including one that was cracked) and discovered they were laminated! There was a piece of plastic in between two pieces of glass. This prevented the cracked piece from just coming apart, thank goodness! Finding new pieces of laminated glass for the wind screen would have been incredibly expensive, if I could have found them at all!

Then there was the matter of the engine. The boat without any kind of engine would be worth a lot less. Even a 60-year-old two stroke would have added value. So I pulled the boat up to my son's house in Loveland. He is a Mechanical Engineer and loved to mess with engines. This beast was like nothing he'd ever seen, of course, being mostly a car guy. First we checked compression and amazingly it was all pretty darn good. Then we got some new plugs and he rigged up a system to get fuel into the carbs. After some twiddling and adjusting, we actually got the thing to run! We weren't in the water so we couldn't run it for more than about 20 seconds, but we took a video of it working and called it a day. He was highly pleased with himself. Me too!

Finally, I put everything back together, using a bunch of new stainless-steel hardware. Much of the old hardware was not stainless and had rotted away to nothing. I had not done anything to the hull, which had some scratches, but the interior was amazingly original and in great shape. I put her on the market for $7,500 and crossed my fingers. I was hoping someone who had grown up with one of these would spy it and come running. How right I was!

The ad got no hits for a couple of weeks, so I reduced the price to $7000. I really expected people from either the east or west coast to be more interested in a time capsule like this, but it turned out to be a guy just a couple of miles away in southeast Denver. He had grown up in New England and just like I'd hoped, his family had this exact boat when he was a kid. I could see the twinkle in his eye when he first saw her, but like most things, it was not going to be easy. A boat purchase was not in his budget and he was going to get in trouble with his wife. We parted ways and I thought it was a lost deal. Then a couple weeks later he came back and offered $6,500 which I quickly accepted. A

$3500 profit was a substantial contribution for an organization that survived off charitable donations and volunteers.

* * *

My next job for CSC was making some new daggerboards for their Optimists. These were very simple – basically a straight piece of ¾" plywood with a slight bevel at the front and back and a couple of pieces of 1x2 at the top so one could lift it out of the water and keep it from falling through the daggerboard slot. I made two stupid errors on these. First, I used regular plywood (rather than marine plywood, which uses better glue for a marine environment) and didn't pay attention to the grain, so I cut the boards with the grain running side to side down, rather than up and down, which would be stronger if something was hit. Kids ran into things on the bottom all the time! So these boards did not last very long.

The second was one of the most hilarious and stupid errors I've ever made in any DIY project. I started with a large piece of plywood and the daggerboards were about 32" long, so I had to make a cut from side to side that long. I was actually recording my work on this project with my GoPro. I had the plywood on the end of my folding table I used for working outside. I carefully measured and cut through with my circular saw as I didn't have a table saw. When the cut piece fell to the driveway, I realized I had also cut about 2" off the end of my table! I hadn't felt the saw going through the thin aluminum and plastic of the table. Knowing I was recording, I kept the swearing to PG levels, went and got the camera and showed the world my stupidity. It was actually pretty funny. I should send the video into America's Funniest Home Videos.

The next big CSC project was another batch of old daggerboards and rudders/tillers that needed refurbishment. Many were originally varnished, which had worn off long ago. Rather than trying to bring the wood back to life, I decided to paint them, using the same technique I had with the first Whaler. Lots of sanding, epoxy repair where needed, primer coat, then two coats of quality paint. I also applied some sheets of fiberglass to a couple of the worst pieces.

I once again needed a couple of new daggerboards and one rudder which was so warped it was unusable. This time I hunted down a 4 X 8 sheet of marine plywood, which was not an easy task in land locked Colorado! It was also $150! But these ended up looking pretty good and have held up for the last several years.

My most recent project was another 13' Whaler whose fiberglass was in mostly really good condition, but the wood was in terrible shape. Once again, I decided to paint instead of varnish or wood oil. Some of the wood was so weathered it would never have come back to life. This little Whaler had a console, which was rare on the smaller boats. Taking all the wood off took over 6 hours, with much swearing at previous owners who had not used stainless steel screws. The old screws would strip, and I'd have to get my Dremel tool out to cut a grove in the top and use a flat bladed screwdriver to slowly wind it out by hand, rather than my much faster drill/driver. It was so time consuming and frustrating. But I eventually got them all out and followed my now proven process as described above. Some of the boards were so weathered that there were deep grooves in the grain that I filled with thickened epoxy and then sanded smooth. (Or as smoothly as possible.) I assumed putting it all back together would be easier than taking apart, but I was wrong. With some of the holes now covered up, it was harder to see how things lined up perfectly. In the end, I got it done and felt good about another excellent result.

One of the big money makers for CSC are summer camps. They take kids from about 8 all the way up to teenagers. They go out in their respective fleets with a coach boat (The Whalers) or two and run through exercises and little races. It's a lot of fun to watch them learn new skills and some of them are pretty impressive. One thing they teach early on is how to recover from a capsize, as well as how to purposefully capsize the boat. When they are between activities or just fooling around in dead air, the kids will capsize their boat by pulling the main over, stepping on the edge of the boat, then as it starts to come over on top of them, they sling a leg over the high side and step on the daggerboard which is now horizontal. If they push down, the boat comes back up. I've watched kids do this over and over. Pretty cool!

CSC has been an important part of my sailing over the last few years, and I am extremely grateful they rejuvenated my sailing interest. I have been able to give back to them in the form of several hundred volunteer hours, purchasing all of the materials used out of my own pocket and some financial contributions.

It should also be mentioned that the organization has a couple of paid employees, but much of the rest of their activities are run and supported by volunteers at all levels. While I have been volunteering, there have been two Directors and both are amazing people, full of energy and kindness for both the kids and helpers. The one Director who retired became a realtor and helped Kathy and me find our new home, and has become a good friend.

Chapter Eleven

The Blizzard Charter

In 2014, I moved in with Kathy and her three kids: Luka, Payton, and Dakota. Shortly thereafter, we bought a home in SE Denver, not far from Cherry Creek Reservoir, one of the popular lakes around Denver. Her kids were 8, 12, and 16 at the time, while my own were grown and out of the house. Kathy was not a sailor, but I hoped to do a better job of introducing her to my favorite pastime than I had done with my son.

By 2021, I had long wanted to charter my own boat as an adult, but not having any real big boat experience, most charter companies wouldn't let me. We also had a problem in that Luka couldn't leave the country without his father's consent until he was 16 – and there was no communication between them. So, that meant chartering in the U.S. I also wanted to find a situation that would give me some training before going out on our own. I found just the place on the southwest coast of Florida, with a charter company that was also a sailing school, and had a few boats for charter.

This was not like Sunsail or The Moorings, with hundreds of boats all around the world. This was a small-time operation, with just one larger boat, a 2008 Seawind 1000XL catamaran. Seawinds have long been at the top of my list for cruising cats, with a nice combination of space and performance. The 1000XL was just over 35' in total length and a beam of 19'. There were four double cabins in total, a single head, and a large galley that took up most of the starboard hull. There was a forepeak forward and a separate double cabin aft of the galley. The port hull had the head at the stern, the primary cabin midships, and another V-berth forward. Frankly, not a single one of the double cabins could really sleep two people, as we later found out.

An oddity with this design was that there was not a properly enclosed salon. Rather, it was open to the cockpit, with a large table forward and a bench across the stern, with the "Aussie grill" in the middle. (I would have much preferred the grill on one side or the other, so someone could lay down.) This boat had double Yamaha 9.9 HP outboards that you sat on as the steering positions on both sides. The outboards lifted under way, which was a nice feature. For a boat that weighed around 12,000 pounds, these engines seemed to be fine, although it was a little noisy in the cockpit.

There were two steering wheels; you had to look through the salon's main windows or peek around the outside of the cabin top to see forward. There was a huge main and tiny, self tacking, roller furler jib. The owner had reduced the size of the jib to provide a bigger cushion for untrained sailors when they were in stronger breezes. Capsizing one of these boats would be extremely hard, but they don't give much warning when they do go over. When you have charterers of variable experience, you want to give them more leeway to survive a mistake. And a mistake in this case could involve a capsize, if too much sail was up in an unexpected blow. In a monohull, the boat will keep heeling over, letting you know that you need to reduce sail.

Southwest Florida was a cruising ground generally thought of as very nice, but shallow. We had done a trip to North Captiva Island many years before, and it was remote and beautiful, accessible only by boat. Our charter marina was a little further north, but it looked like protected waters, with lots of little places to tuck into at night.

The plan was for a couple of days of training from the charter manager/sailing instructor, then we'd be on our own for a couple of days. Then, we'd planned a day in Fort Myers at the end to play tourists. There were two fees, one for the charter and one for the instruction. I assumed he would take over a cabin for a night or two as we learned how to handle the boat.

The crew was Kathy, her oldest daughter Dakota, and youngest child, Luka. Payton was living in New York City and unable to join us. Since I was really the only one with any sailing experience, I would be skipper, cook, and head bottle washer. To be fair, they all caught on quickly and seemed to enjoy working together docking, anchoring, raising sails, etc. We also shared cooking duties.

* * *

This March trip started out badly, as Denver had one of its worst snowstorms in decades, with 20" of snow falling in 24 hours; the drifts were quite a bit higher. Our direct flight to Fort Myers was to leave in the morning, but everything was cancelled coming or going. So, we started scrambling to see what other options were available. The direct flight from Denver was just once a day, so we had to find a way to go through another city. Many frustrating hours of sitting on hold netted us a flight through Houston leaving at about 3:00 p.m. and a connector to Fort Myers the next day.

The roads were still a mess and we ended up barely making our flight, even though we left hours ahead of time. The main road to DIA was virtually closed, so we tried to take back roads and that ended up worse. When we finally got to the parking lot, it had not been plowed. So, we had to dig out a parking space, then drag our suitcases through slush and snow to the terminal. Everyone's feet were soaked by the time we got there!

We spent a night in a motel in Houston, then got into Fort Myers the next day midafternoon, where our Uber was waiting. Somehow, we had not communicated our problems well enough and she had showed up at the airport the previous day. She charged us for the wasted trip anyhow.

We finally got to the boat around 5:00 p.m., after stopping for groceries for the next few days along the way. Our charter manager gave us a quick tour of the boat. We put our things away and pushed off to do a little practicing in the harbor. He wanted to see how I handled the boat. Of course, I'd read tons in anticipation and understood the advantage of having two engines 12' apart. It was a breeze to spin the boat in her length, with careful throttle control. We then left the harbor and he went through how to raise sails and drop the anchor, and conducted some other safety checks. When we returned, he said we were good to go and left.

While I'd thought we were going to get a couple of days of instruction, he was apparently happy with what he saw. This was a little frustrating, as the instruction fee was substantial, about $1,600. I should have raised an objection at that time, at least to get clarification of what we were paying for. But frankly, we were happy to be on our own and ready to start our adventure, after a VERY long and stressful couple of days.

The next day dawned warm and sunny, but a nasty surprise awaited us when we went to make our first breakfast. All the dry food had been invaded by ants! There were traps around but were obviously inadequate, and much of the fresh food we had bought the day before was ruined. So, we had to throw a great deal of the food away. We called the charter manager, and he came right over with some spray. We borrowed a huge plastic cooler from the marina and stored the dry food in there for the remainder of the trip. The boat had both a top-loading freezer easily capable of storing enough food for four people for a week, and a separate fridge. The galley was and is one of the best in a smaller yacht, with loads of storage space and huge counters running both sides of the starboard hull.

* * *

We finally pushed off after having lunch in the little café on shore. We got sails up and had a nice sail down Gasparilla Sound in 10 to 12 knots and flat seas. We were heading toward Caya Costa State Park, which has one of the best protected anchorages along the whole coast, with small entrances on both the north and south ends. Surrounded by low mangroves, it was a perfect place for our first night. Anchor holding was good, although we missed on our first try. Fortunately, I noticed we were dragging and we got it right on the second try.

It was quite warm, so we tried a swim in the rather muddy-looking water. The wind was blowing pretty hard now, and we were getting blown away from the boat. So, I threw a line in, and we broke out the old orange PFDs to use as floaties. The water was a bit chilly but refreshing, and we had a good time. I'd bought a nice piece of fish at the grocery store and even though I was the only one excited about it, I was determined to have a good fish dinner while we were in Florida! I put it on the "barbie" with some lemon, salt, and pepper, and even the non-fish lovers seemed to enjoy it. The sunset was epic, with a classic fireball slowly dipping into the ocean behind Cayo Costa. It was a brilliant end to a great day.

Kathy and I had discovered the night before that the fore and aft doubles were completely inadequate for two adults, so I moved to the port V-berth. At MAYBE 48" wide, there was no way for us to get comfortable, even for a couple of not very large people who like to cuddle. Both of us were a lot more comfortable apart. In later versions of this boat, this berth has been turned 90° and is now a true queen. It is much more practical, and probably one of the best berths in a yacht under 40'.

We had been noticing a bad smell, and while the boat had a holding tank for the head, I was concerned something was off. I looked at the plumbing from the head to the tank and nothing looked amiss. When we flushed the head, we could definitely smell a poopy smell at the stern of the boat. I called the manager and discussed it with him. After a little time spent trouble-shooting, he hung up and called the owner. It turned out the owner had filled the holding tank with water and vinegar to clean it out and had not emptied it! So, what we had been smelling was the overflow vent from the holding tank, which was above the water line near the stern.

Now, we had a problem of what to do with a full holding tank. We were not in a marina, and didn't want to go back to Burnt Store. The nearest marina was Boca Grande, a few miles north across the cut in the barrier islands from Gasparilla Sound out to the Gulf of Mexico. So, we headed over there, with a pretty stiff wind at our back. With only 45 minutes or so to go, we left the sails down and motored. As we approached the entrance, a 130' motor yacht came in from the Gulf, powered around us, and beat us to the dock by about 10 minutes. I thought it was a dick move; the small marina's guest dock was completely taken up by this giant yacht. I radioed and asked how long they thought he'd be, and was told it would be hours. Swear words!

So, we headed to our next destination for the night, Cabbage Key, about seven miles the other direction (south). We were now heading directly into the wind, so kept the engines going. A boat is not allowed to empty a holding tank close to shore: you're supposed to be at least three miles off shore. That would have involved going out into the Gulf, which frankly was looking pretty rough and would have taken a couple of hours at least. Let's just say that the skipper made a decision to take care of the problem before we reached our next port. I figured it was mostly water, with a bit of vinegar and a little bit of sludge.

* * *

Cabbage Key is a small resort hotel, restaurant, and marina on a private island north of Fort Myers. Besides a guest house, there are rental cottages scattered around the property. There's also a nice walking path around the island on hard packed sand, with many points of interest and history posted on little plaques along the way. You stroll through a pretty dense forest, with lots of wildlife and birds. On the hotel grounds are some old turtles who make their homes in the gardens. The marina can accommodate about 25 boats, and access is through a tight channel. The whole place is completely charming and a throwback to "old Florida."

When we arrived, they put us on the end of a pier, and I expertly backed us into the spot. I was nervous as this was really the first time I had docked the boat, and while the theory of twin engines and amazing control sounds good, in practice it was a large yacht. As it turned out, our 50' shore power line would not reach their access point (even though the dock guy said it would), so we had to move to another spot. I was not so successful this time, coming in too fast. 12,000 pounds isn't a lot for a cruising cat, but it carried a lot more momentum than my 1,400-pound boat! Luckily, lots of helpful hands brought us to a quick stop.

There were real showers on shore, so we bundled up our bath stuff and went up. They were not very nice, badly in need of a remodel and lots of cleaning, but at least we were clean and refreshed. I had made a dinner reservation at the hotel restaurant and we were looking forward to letting someone else cook. The meal and service were amazing, and I had my chance to have a really good fish dinner prepared by an expert. Everyone was likewise pleased with their meals, and the adults had a cocktail or two. Completely happy, we made our way to bed.

At about midnight, I awoke to the sound of voices and feet on the deck above me. It was a couple of boys, probably about 12 years old, who were out fishing. They'd caught one of their lines on the bow of the boat and were trying to get it free. I stuck my head out of the forward hatch and barked at them to get the heck home and stop bothering people in the middle of the night. I know I scared the crap out them, as they jumped in surprise, then scurried away. I had to wonder what parents would let their youngsters wander around at midnight? The other surprise was that a cold front had come through and our normally comfortable bedtime temperatures were suddenly 20 degrees cooler. We wrapped up in all of our clothes, scrounged for extra blankets and towels, and tried to keep warm.

* * *

The next day, we got up slowly and had a relaxed breakfast. The wind had done a complete 180, and was now coming from the north. So once again, we would be going right into it. With nowhere in particular to go, I started tacking up the channel in about 15 knots of breeze. It was really only the second good sail, and I was enjoying the warm temperatures and good breeze. The Seawind did not sail very close to the wind, and we were probably tacking through more than 90°, but we were in no hurry. There were many beautiful homes along some shorelines, while others were covered in mangroves. The scenery was nice. The self-tacking jib meant I could sail the boat on my own, and Kathy and the kids could read or snooze.

The original schedule was that Cabbage Key would be our last stop. Since we had arrived a day late, we asked the manager if we could have another night. He didn't have another charter behind us, so agreed. We thought about going back to Boca Grande for the night, but after our experience with them, we decided to go back to Cayo Costa. I'd also wanted to try anchoring on the west (Gulf) side of Cayo Costa, but it was quite exposed and really needed the wind to be from the east. Any other direction would be too exposed.

We came into Cayo Costa from the north which, according to the charts, was very shallow and narrow. One of the benefits of a cruising cat is shallow non-displacement keels. Our 36' boat only had a draft of 39". I carefully threaded our way into the north end of the anchorage, fretfully watching the chartplotter. And sure enough, right where it said we had a chance, I could feel the boat start to slow down as the port keel dug into the sand. Feeling that it wasn't a hard grounding and suspecting it would not be long, I gunned both engines and powered through to deeper water. It was perhaps not a very smart idea as, if we had gone hard aground, we would have had a real problem trying to get off. Unlike a monohull, which can be heeled to reduce draft, the only way to get through the sand would be to get pulled out. Fortunately for me, my hunch was right.

We returned to our same spot as the first night, and this time executed the anchoring technique perfectly. The crew were getting the hang of it! We'd shown up midafternoon, so had a nap, and enjoyed the peace and quiet of the location. The wind was piping up and it was warm and sunny, like it had been all week. Kathy cooked a magnificent spaghetti dinner and we went to bed early, knowing that we had to get the boat back to its home base around noon in order to make our flight.

* * *

There is something particularly sad about the last day of a charter. You have to pack and get ready to go home and, unless it's been a disaster, no one wants to leave. I've never been on a charter when I didn't have this feeling on the last day. We'd had an amazing time and seen a couple of very nice places. It felt like a million miles away from our jobs and reality back home in Colorado. Time seemed to have slowed to a crawl, and the five days we were gone felt like weeks. Being in charge of the boat ourselves felt like a real accomplishment for a rookie skipper and newbie crew. They really enjoyed pitching in together and feeling like they were working as a team. By the end of the trip, they had settled into roles they were comfortable with.

Unfortunately, the last day's sail was disappointing. We had about 10 miles to go. The winds started out light at around 5 knots, then kept going down, until we motor sailed the last few miles. We were to go to the pump-out location and I once again came in too fast, and we had to fend off the dock. Obviously, I needed more practice! The charter manager was there to meet us. While the normal procedure was to charge for the pump-out of the holding tank, he generously (sarcasm intended) offered to waive the cost (about $40). Frankly, I thought he should have offered a lot more than that.

We'd arranged for our Uber to pick us up about 2:00 p.m., so we had a little time to chat with the manager and discuss various things, including the way the whole "instruction" thing had come down. I had been stressing about it for the last few days, feeling like I had not received the value I'd paid for. But realizing I was not really in a position to re-negotiate our agreement, I knew I probably couldn't ask for a refund at this point. (Charter fees are paid 100% up front.) I did broach the issue with the manager, and after some confusion, he seemed to understand my point of view. He suggested if we came back, we could have one free night, which was something at least. But I knew the chances of coming back to this area were very slim. The whole point was to get experience, so we could go to the Bahamas or the BVI in the future.

It was a somber cab ride to the airport, but at least the direct flight home went without a hitch. We arrived home to greet our very happy dogs on time.

* * *

Lessons learned and impressions from this trip. You may notice I have not mentioned either the charter company or the charter manager's name. Since I felt like we were taken advantage of to a certain degree, I don't want to disparage what was overall a really fun trip. I will make sure I understand what is being offered and will get it in writing in the future. I assumed I knew what the instruction involved, and didn't think for a minute that he would cut the whole thing short and let us go. I should have thought about that as a possibility and insisted some sort of financial adjustment be made, if the instruction terms changed.

This is a great cruising area that we barely scratched the surface of. We could have gone south at least another 10 miles to Fort Myers, along Pine Island Sound and north another 10 miles in the other direction to Placida – not to mention the Gasparilla Sound/Charlotte Harbor area.

March was a great time of year to visit, with sunny, warm days, cool nights, few bugs, and steady breezes. The area is nicely protected, with lots of small coves and harbors to explore. It was a perfect first-time location for newbies with no sailing experience. We never had waves over about 18", and staying inside the barrier islands meant it was always pretty calm. Starting on a cruising cat meant no heeling either. The area IS very shallow, and a deep keel monohull would have fewer anchoring options. Our 39" draft meant we could go just about anywhere.

But if you're looking for beautiful, clear water, this is the wrong side of the state. The Gulf water is probably clearer, but also going to be a lot rougher, with far fewer anchoring and gunkholing options. If you want crystal-clear water suitable for snorkeling or diving, the East Coast is better, and you can't beat the Caribbean or the Bahamas.

Would I go again? Yes, but not before visiting the aforementioned locations.

Chapter Twelve
Shenanigans

I have always been fascinated with multihulls, catamarans, and trimarans. One day on the Solent as a kid, a 60' (huge for the time) Newick trimaran was making its way out to sea and it just looked surreal, like a huge bird with massive amas, or float hulls. The akas or crossbeams were beautifully curved. It glided noiselessly and effortlessly along, reaching speeds we could not even dream of in our 30' cruising monohull.

After my racing days on Santana 22s and 20s and J-24s and other small keel boats came to an end, I became interested in the speed potential and stability of these boats. Ian Farrier was an Aussie who came up with a clever and brilliant folding design for trimarans. They allowed the amas, or float hulls, to be folded up against the main hull for transporting on regular road trailers. Since trimarans get their stability from the amas and not a big keel, the boats are generally lighter than comparably sized monohulls. A lot of Farrier's designs had been built by home builders, custom builders, and by Corsair, who'd sold a couple of thousand Corsairs ranging from 20' up to about 37'.

Before Farrier went into business with Corsair, he sold plans for his boats and built a few smaller examples in the 18' to 22' range. He tested his ideas with these boats. They were the Tramp, Super Tramp, Ostac and a couple of others. Many were built in Australia, and some in the U.S. When he joined forces with Corsair, the first boat they introduced was a 27-footer called the F27. It had a small aft cabin, a reasonable main cabin, a forepeak, and a head. Accommodations were cramped for a 27' boat – more like a 23' or 24' – but this was part of the compromise of having a boat that weighed under 4000 pounds that could be trailered with a mid-sized truck or SUV, and could reach speeds in the high teens with the right sails and crew. Low to mid teens were also easily possible, with a less competent crew. This compares to the maximum speed of 6 to 7 knots for most cruising monohulls under 40'.

Also in my mind was my new girlfriend, Kathy. She was not a sailor, and knowing how heeling can freak some people out, I thought a boat that could barely heel would be a great way to introduce her to sailing. By this time, my kids were grown and out of the house, but she still had two at home, also non-sailors. As it turned out, it was a good choice from that standpoint.

Around 2014, I started looking at the options available for smaller trimarans. At that time, the smallest being built by Corsair was the Pulse 600. At about 20', it had no accommodations, but was designed as a day sailer and racer. Even used, they were running $35,000 or more, which was way out of my range. Windrider was an interesting builder, making their boats out of rotomolded plastic, like modern kayaks. This made them virtually indestructible and cheap to build. They made three sizes: the 17' looked to be a good size, with forward seating for two. At the time, my Dad had quit sailing and was quite frail; I thought this might be a good way for him to get on the water safely. I floated the idea to my parents and they were amenable.

The boat was 17' long and had two forward facing seats, one for the skipper and one for the passenger. All controls led back to the rear seat, so the main and jib could both be controlled by the skipper. The jib was on a roller furler and main had a standard bolt rope for the luff. Steering was done with your feet, with a simple cable system running to the rudder at the very stern of the boat. The amas had no storage and there were nice nets on either side for passengers to sit on. There was a reasonable amount of leg space for both people, but you definitely sat down in the boat rather than on it. As I was to find out, there wasn't much wiggle room.

I did a demo sail on a WR17 at a Denver-area lake and was very impressed. It was easy to sail and clearly had a good turn of speed, even in light airs. We ordered a brand-new boat (2014) from the factory, with virtually every option on the list. It was $14,500, plus another $1,000 or so for delivery.

* * *

There were problems right from the start. Setting the boat up was not without frustration. The factory instructions were not very good at the time, although they later made several videos that helped a lot. Raising the substantial mast was NOT as easy as they made it appear. The guy they used in their videos was young and tall, and he made it look easy. It's really a two-person job. I tried to design a system to help raise the mast alone, but it never really worked.

I ordered the "storage system," which was several cloth pockets and shelves to help stow stuff away. There were no instructions. There was a storage shelf that fit in the pointy end of the bow. This should have been installed at the factory, as it took a real contortionist act to get it installed. I am not large at 5' 9" and 180 pounds, and I barely fit. It was claustrophobic and unpleasant. The holes for the steering post were not drilled out, so I had to do that. Same for one of the ama pins. The trampoline (net) lines were missing and there were no instructions of any kind sent with the boat; they were emailed later. Then in the instructions, many pictures of parts did not match what was sent to me.

The factory trailer did not have a trailer jack or spare, nor were they offered as options. The trailer came with a broken brake light lens that I had to replace via mail. I ordered forward hand steering, which I didn't get; what I did get was the parts for forward foot steering, which I hadn't ordered. I never received the parts for the forward steering. I ordered a screecher, which came with no instructions. One of the screws to fasten the forward end of the floor was rolling around in the bottom of the boat.

The lack of attention to detail was astonishing. Obviously, they did not set up each boat before delivery, hence they did not uncover the mistakes others made in terms of items left out, holes misaligned, sloppy workmanship, etc. There were probably five or six additional shipments that had to be made from the factory, as well as numerous emails with instructions, added information, clarification, etc. It's no wonder boat builders can't make money! I was absolutely shocked at how a manufacturer could put out a product that apparently had virtually no quality checks or controls.

The good: the boat's performance was good, at least for an old monohuller like me. (I wonder if someone more familiar with multihulls would have been as impressed?) I saw 11.2 MPH on my handheld GPS, and it was frequently over 10 MPH. The trampolines were a great place for the kids, as long as they didn't mind getting a little wet in over 6 or 7 knots of wind. Cockpit lead controls were well-laid out and super easy to operate.

The quality of the entire boat was very good, and excellent hardware was used throughout. The rotomolded plastic was extremely tough, if not very attractive. The sails themselves were quality, and the roller furling worked well. A great deal of thought was put into maximizing storage, and their "storage system" offered a lot of little pockets for organization of the small cockpit.

The bad: they made a big deal about the forward facing and foot steering. I hated both – a lot. The seat was not comfortable for more than about an hour, even after trying a variety of cushions. The seat back didn't adjust, so it was hard to find the right position. The seat base did move fore and aft, so accommodated people of different heights. I imagine if you were fuller figured, you would not be comfortable at all and would find it difficult to get in and out.

The foot steering locked your legs and feet in place, and it was quite difficult to make small steering adjustments. I found that my feet and calves cramped after a fairly short period of time. I MUCH preferred a real cockpit and tiller, and the ability to move around, adjust my position, etc. Sitting facing forward, you had to balance the boat as it heeled, straining your neck and back since you couldn't actually lean very much. So, besides my ass going numb, legs cramping, and having a general lack of steering feeling, it was great! Being able to move around and have precise control is far superior to being stuck in the bucket seat, unable to easily move.

Getting out of the seat took several seconds and a bit of athleticism. If you needed to get to something quickly, you couldn't. Or do something quickly, like docking. You had to stay in your seat so you could steer, then wiggle out and dance across the tramps to the amas to come alongside a dock. If you missed the dock, you'd have to get back in the seat to get going again. What a pain. At only 400 pounds, the boat carried no momentum, and judging how fast you were going to get to the dock without thumping it was difficult. I never did figure it out.

The outboard motor mount sat to the driver's left. I used a Minn Kota 40 with a full-size battery that fit nicely behind the seat. (Although that was not the best place for it, from a weight distribution standpoint.) It was convenient and moved the boat surprisingly well. I saw 4.5 knots in flat water at full speed. The problem was, on a starboard tack in breeze (12+ knots), the left ama would dip low enough to drag the motor mount in the water, bringing a bucketful into the driver's lap! And since you couldn't really move to jump out of the way, you were getting the full douse every time. So now, not only were you stuck in one place, but you were wet as well.

The amas slid in and out on tubes. There was an inherent sloppiness in this arrangement, with the side stays attaching to the amas. The rig is not adjustable except by moving pins on the side stays, so getting the rig tight was something that really needed to happen on shore. (But no suggestions from the factory about how tight or which holes to use were provided.) I tried making adjustments in the water at the dock, using the main halyard to pull the amas up, but could only move one notch, or less than an inch. I suspect it was off by at least 2" on either side. This would need to have been achieved on shore with at least one extra person, as one would have to lift the ama and the other move the shroud pin.

As the boat came from the factory, the forestay was far too loose, so as it went through waves, the mast moved all over the place. This is also a result of the side stays not being tight enough. This destroyed sail shape and everything bounced around. With a saggy forestay, it didn't point worth a hoot. This again needed some factory direction. Having come from the J-24 world, where there were tuning guides the size of small books, having NOTHING to go by was frustrating. So, sailing back and forth on a reach was fun, but going to weather wasn't. It was kind of like driving a fast car in third gear and only being able to go in a straight line – no fun in the corners!

* * *

I ended up selling the WR17 after two seasons to a local guy for $9500, losing over $5,000. With new ones going for around $10,000 base price, it was hard to justify asking more than that, even with all the extras. He already owned one, so got a screaming deal on a boat that was virtually new.

However, it gave me a taste for trimarans, and I kept thinking about what other options there were. I looked pretty seriously at Richard Woods' site. He had designed cats and tris for decades and sold the plans to mostly home builders, who would construct them of plywood and epoxy. Some of his designs were very sophisticated and over 30', which sounds like a giant project for a home builder.

But he also had some simpler designs, including a line of trimarans from 10' to 20' designed with a folding mechanism. One design, called a Strike, was 18' with a small, protected cabin area and large cockpit. It was intended to be built using a beach cat for the ama hulls and rig. This greatly reduced the cost and build time, since the only thing to build was the main hull. It was a brilliant design, although not a very beautiful boat. The cabin roof was quite bulky and ruined the lines of the boat.

I actually bought study plans for the Strike, which had a lot of detail about how the boat goes together. It also had a complete materials list, so I could figure out how much materials would cost. Besides the cost of the donor beach cat, it would have been about $3,000 plus, according to Richard, a couple of hundred hours of labor. My suspicion was that it would take a great deal more time than that, but he could probably knock one out that fast. I was also pretty sure that knowing every little mistake and mishap made during the build process would ruin the sense of pride of actually constructing one.

Ultimately, I decided against it, since I didn't have a suitable shop to build it in. It would barely fit in a standard-length garage, but occupy the space for months – or years. Plus, what would I do about a trailer? There were a couple of good YouTube channels that showed the build process and it didn't seem all that difficult. But…

At the same time, I was trying to find something already built, and found that small trimarans were as scarce as hen's teeth. There were a few home builds from other designers; I actually found a Strike 18 for sale in Canada, but it sold before I could get serious about it. There were a couple of Farrier-designed Tramps around, and I started to focus my search on these.

* * *

Built in the mid '80s, both in Australia and the U.S., they are 20' long with a 14' 9" beam, and use the genius folding ama system now found on all Farrier/Corsair boats. There's no cabin, so no accommodation, sink, or head. There is a little protected space at the forward end of the huge cockpit. It has a good-sized storage locker forward as well as another one aft behind the cockpit. There are two sail plans: a regular Tramp with a 26' mast, and a Super Tramp with a 30' mast and running backstays. I have always found the name amusing, as Super Tramp is also one of my all-time favorite bands.

Ian Farrier was not afraid to use a little hyperbole in his advertising and claimed the boat was suitable for camping for four under a cockpit tent. I have no idea where four people would sleep in the cockpit – perhaps utilizing the nets? He had a hilarious picture of someone using a portable head in the forward storage space, with their head sticking out of the hatch. He also claimed the boat could achieve speeds in the high teens, but I think you would be on the edge of disaster at that point. You would have to be in "hair on fire" conditions to reach those speeds. Speeds in the low teens were much more likely, on a beam reach and flat water.

The boat is heavy at 1,400 pounds and has about 230 square feet of sail area standard. The much larger Corsair F24 is about 1,800 pounds and has a lot more sail. The much newer Corsair Pulse 600 has almost the same dimensions but under 1,000 pounds and almost 300 square feet of sail. The Pulse really is a rocket ship.

A Super Tramp came up for sale in northern Florida, around Edgewater. It looked in decent-enough shape, but had been painted yellow. The trailer looked good, and there was a 5 HP Honda outboard as well. There was a jib and main that were original, and a slightly larger genoa of unknown brand and age. The seller, David, was not using the boat and had paid $9,000 a couple of years earlier. He was offering it at $7,000, which I thought was a reasonable price. We agreed on a $500 deposit to hold the boat. He'd had another offer at $5,000, which was then increased by the same buyer to $6,000, which I thought was silly. The boats were SO scarce that playing games on the price for a good one didn't seem like a wise strategy. Someone who could afford $6,000 could afford $7,000. I was lucky the other buyer wasn't more sensible in his negotiations.

The seller really wanted me to look at it before making a final decision, which I found odd. My dad and I had bought and sold 13 boats, and never went to see them in person before making the deal. As camera phones were more and more prevalent, getting good video was pretty easy. I actually did a VHS recording of one boat I was selling, and sent it to the potential buyer. Maybe we were naïve or just plain dumb, but we were never disappointed.

This boat was about as far away from me in the country as one could get but I agreed, and booked a plane ticket to Orlando. David picked me up at the airport, and we had a nice chat on the way to his place on the coast. He also treated me to a delicious fish lunch, one of the things I really miss about living in Colorado. It was in a nice roadside restaurant on a beautiful estuary, and we ate outside in perfect 80° weather – lovely.

The boat was as advertised, with the only real drawback being the obnoxiously bright yellow color, which was everywhere except inside the lockers. The quality of the paint job seemed decent enough, although there were some rough spots. Kathy insisted I change the color, which ended up being a mess – and another story. David turned out to be a lovely man in his early 70s who had kind of grown out of the boat. Of course, he had piles of extra gear, fenders, lines, and hardware, which all came with the boat.

* * *

This was February, and it was not practical to drive cross country to get the boat for at least a couple of months. I also preferred to have a co-pilot, so Kathy's oldest daughter, Dakota, agreed to come with me. This was 2020, and COVID was taking off in the country, making travel very different from even a few months earlier.

The next decision was which vehicle to take. We had a Chevy Colorado pickup truck with the 5 cylinder 3.7 liter engine and hitch. It was a nice enough small truck, but didn't have much power and would not be very comfortable for a fast cross-country trip. We also had a Toyota Sienna minivan with the 3.5 liter V6, which I decided was preferable, so had a hitch installed. The boat and trailer were only about 2,200 pounds, so it wasn't a lot of weight to pull. The minivan also had a decent rear seat suitable for taking naps during the day. We removed one of the second-row seats for extra interior space.

Our trip out was uneventful. It was great to have someone along to talk to and take the occasional spell at the wheel. Dakota was smart, thoughtful, and curious, and we thoroughly enjoyed our time together. We solved all the problems of the world in those five days. We split the trip into two nights coming and going, and one night there. One advantage of traveling during COVID was that no one else was, so hotels were cheap and empty, sometimes disturbingly so.

We arrived midday on the third day, and met David to check out the boat. I gave him the balance of the money and agreed we would collect the boat in the morning, then be on our way. My good friend Beth (Also the Editor for this book.) was living in St. Augustine, about an hour north, so she met Dakota and me for dinner. Another delicious fish dinner for Mike! We hadn't seen each other in a long time, so it was great to catch up.

We didn't have a spare tire, but there was a trailer place down the road that sold us one for $20 the next morning. Next, we went to David's house to pick up the rest of the gear, sails, outboard, etc. Then, we hit the road and were on our way home. Dakota was initially a bit nervous about towing, but soon got used to it. There were no plates on the trailer, which provided for some nervous episodes with a couple of cops along the way. But we were never pulled over.

The trip home was uneventful, except for one thing. At a truck stop midday on day one, I checked the trailer and discovered a bolt from one of the bunk boards was missing, and the bracket was millimeters away from making a hole in the hull. Fortunately, I'd brought a good stash of hardware and tools with me, and had the perfect bolt for it. Crisis averted.

Our gas mileage was predictably poor. The van only got about 23 MPG on the highway without a trailer; with the boat, we ranged from 15 ½ all the way down to about 11. Still, that was a lot better than it could have been with a larger vehicle. The Sienna turned out to be the perfect tow vehicle. It was quiet and smooth, and wasn't really affected by having the trailer behind it. We kept it around 70 MPH, and it was quite happy at that speed. There was tons of room inside, even with all the extra gear, sails, OB, etc. We got back to Denver late on the afternoon of day five.

CHERRY CREEK RESERVOIR

I had reserved a slip at (ironically named) Pelican Bay Marina on Cherry Creek Reservoir, about 10 minutes from our home in SE Denver. It's a nice marina with about 180 slips, surprising for a lake of its size. The reservoir was only about 800 acres and about a mile and a quarter across in all directions. Quite a large section of the east end of the reservoir was very shallow, reducing the effective area even further. And unlike many of Colorado's reservoirs, this one was fed from runoff from the plains, not the mountains, so the water was not very nice. In fact, they frequently had algae blooms in the summer when the air temperatures heated up – as did the water. Large areas of slimy green stuff would close down the beaches. Visibility in the water was virtually nil. I tried to clean the hull bottom from the water and could not see the small skeg at the bottom center of the boat from the surface, about 3' away.

Despite being small, there was LOTS of activity on the lake. There were tons of wakeboard boats and jet skis, as well as an active sailing club. When the wakeboarders and jet skis were out, it made the whole lake miserable for anyone who wanted some peace and quiet. I particularly resented these two groups of power boaters, as they seemed to have little to no common sense as to how their wakes and noise impacted others. The wakeboard guys seemed to love to grind past 50 yards away, creating 3' waves that would throw my little boat around. The jet ski guys must have thought it great fun to blast past also 50 yards away, at 30 knots.

I have never figured out the attraction of either of these types of watercraft. I rented a jet ski on a vacation and was bored after about five minutes. The wakeboarders either fall down and are sucking water all day, or inhaling exhaust fumes from the power boat directly in front of them. They also seem to insist on playing music at 10+ all the time, which I don't get. To me, boating is a place for peace and quiet. Finally, those wakeboard boats are stupid expensive, running $200,000 and WAY up.

However, I did have some glorious sailing days when the lake was either mostly fishermen, or just empty. Winds were best in the spring and fall, and could be little to nothing in the summer. Fortunately, the Super Tramp didn't take much to move, and I had some great days ghosting around at 3 to 4 knots while the "lead-bottom boats" struggled to move at all. The powerboaters were less present during the hump seasons as well, making it all the more attractive.

I never tried to race the Super Tramp for a number of reasons, "been there, done that" being #1. It was obvious that with the sails I had, I would not be competitive. I doubted the boat could beat a well-sailed J-24, a boat I knew a bit about. Most racing is done on windward/leeward course, meaning straight up and downwind. This is not a trimaran's forte, as they excel in reaching conditions.

I would need a new main and jib, and probably some sort of screecher, or downwind/reaching sail. That also meant a bowsprit of some sort. And a ton of money. To be fair, they would all be excellent upgrades, racing or not. There are no PHRF ratings for the boat as far as I know. I am sure I would get killed by the rating people, since the larger Corsair and Farrier boats are rated very aggressively and rarely sail to their ratings in mixed fleets.

So, a cruiser she would stay – and still is.

Chapter Thirteen

San Diego to Santa Barbara on Caliente

After buying the Super Tramp, I frequented a sailing forum for Farrier-designed boats, including Corsairs. One day on the forum, there was a post looking for crew to take a large trimaran from San Diego to San Francisco. I had never really been offshore on any boat and jumped at the chance. Greg, the skipper, contacted me back immediately, and gave me some details.

To be honest, the timing was not great. I'd had a problem with a blocked bile duct, which made me sick. Besides a fever, night sweats, and general fatigue, I had terrible, uncontrollable itching all over my body, which kept me awake all night. The fix was something called an ERCP – a procedure where they stick a tube down your throat and through your stomach, then place a stent, or small tube, in the bile duct to expand it. The process actually involves several ERCPs, each time making the tube bigger, to hopefully create a large enough passage that it wouldn't get clogged again. Each procedure required general anesthesia, and I'd had four procedures, with one scheduled right before the trip was supposed to happen. After each procedure, my recovery took longer and longer. I was very tired with no energy, and also felt depressed. The surgery site was also tender for a week or two afterwards. Not a good state of mind before going offshore. But I was determined not to miss this opportunity, and toughed it out anyhow.

The plan was to take Caliente from San Diego to San Francisco, hopping along the California coast. The boat had already made its way down the Mississippi River, across the west end of the Caribbean

Sea, through the Panama Canal, and up the west coast of Mexico. Greg was the delivery skipper along the Mexican coast, with other crew along the way.

I arrived at the boat in San Diego at about 6:30 p.m., as the sun was setting. Greg asked me to stow my gear quickly, as we were going to set off immediately. I had the starboard side of the aft cabin, with a large double berth. My bunkmate Gabe had been there since midday and was already settled in. Gabe was a 39-year-old Spokane, Washington firefighter, very fit and full of confidence. There wasn't much he wasn't ready to take on. He owned a Corsair F27, so was very familiar with trimarans.

Greg was a mid-50s retired marketing executive/entrepreneur, now doing boat deliveries for fun and (some) profit. He owned the largest Corsair/Farrier trimaran made called Ravenswing (check out his YouTube channel), which at 39' was not much smaller than Caliente. Greg had built much of this boat himself, not quite from scratch but close. He was not only a really good sailor, but could fix just about anything. They were excellent crewmates, and Greg definitely knew what he was doing. His own boat was in Mexico, where he kept it for cruising trips.

My first impression of Caliente was that it was big – really big for a trimaran. My little 20-footer was a toy by comparison. Caliente was a 44' (53' with bowsprit) Chris White-designed trimaran called an Explorer that had spent the last 20 years on Lake Michigan doing lots of racing. With a beam of 28', a draft of 6' (board down), and 1,180 square feet upwind sail area, Caliente was a potent racing machine, having done the Chicago to Mac 19 times and won line honors in 2003. She had a PHRF of -3! At about 11,000 pounds, she was lighter than the 36' Seawind catamaran we chartered a couple of years earlier!

Caliente's mast was 65'. Compared to the skinny 30' mast of my own boat, it looked like a tree trunk! There was a small forepeak with a single berth, and a very small pull-down pilot berth above that. Directly aft of that was the head, with a manual toilet and small sink. The main cabin had settees on either side, but only one was long enough to be used for a berth. To starboard was a galley with a two-burner gas stove and oven, and a small double sink. Opposite the galley was the chart table and a fridge (which didn't work; we had a portable fridge/freezer in the cockpit). The cockpit was fully enclosed with an Isinglass enclosure of clear plastic panels. Under the cockpit was the 27 HP Yanmar engine – barely adequate for a boat with as much windage as this. Aft was the best sleeping cabin that I was to share with Gabe, with a full beam berth – although it was a bit short, even for me!

* * *

We pushed off and headed out into San Diego harbor in fading light. Gabe suggested we go through the reefing process in daylight, which was a good idea, as we ended up needing to do it in the dark later. The motor out was quiet, with a beautiful sunset. We discussed safety issues and equipment, and what the general schedule was to be for the next few days. We were to have four-hour watches every 12 hours. I had the 4:00 a.m. to 8:00 a.m. and 4:00 p.m. to 8:00 p.m. watches, as I like to see the sun come up.

We started off to Catalina Island in a couple knots of breeze, full main and the motor running. We stayed up and chatted while Greg made dinner – pasta and green salad. I went to bed about 10:30 p.m. and was roused from a sound sleep at 4:00 a.m. Earplugs helped with the incredible din from the engine room, which was not soundproofed, a couple of feet away. The boat had a very good electronics package, with a full-function B&G chartplotter with AIS and radar. Both of these were well-used, as that area was very busy, with commercial shipping 24 hours a day!

We were hailed on the VHF radio by Warship 24 at about 1 a.m., asking us what our intended course was, as they were coming up quickly from behind. The AIS description was obscured, indicating it was a U.S. Navy ship. Greg was pretty sure they were using us as part of an exercise, as there was PLENTY of room for them to go around. They ended up steaming north through the night and hung around off L.A. Harbor for the whole next day, as we watched them on AIS.

Keeping track of all of the shipping kept me busy. There was almost a full moon and very flat water. At about 5:00 a.m., a huge (948 feet!) cruise ship came up on us on its way to L.A. Harbor, going 22 knots. It passed us about half a mile away, but it felt much closer. It made me nervous, I can tell you! And those things are always lit up like Christmas trees, which made them look bigger than they are.

Around 6:30 a.m., the sun started to rise. While I was capturing the event on my GoPro, we were visited by a huge pod – several dozen – of dolphins, cruising around the boat for five minutes. There is something about dolphins around boats. Their graceful athleticism and playful nature makes them fascinating, especially for a guy from land-locked Colorado!

I made breakfast burritos with potatoes, eggs, onions, bell pepper, and cheese. These were enjoyed by all, and leftovers were saved for later in the week. In fact, I think Gabe ate four of them, which I took as a compliment. We were approaching Avalon on Catalina Island and diverted to get a better look.

Another huge cruise ship pulled into the harbor at the same time and spoiled the view, but you could tell it was a pretty spectacular place. We cruised up the east side of the island, which took most of the day. Five knots was the comfortable cruising speed under engine for this huge, fast trimaran. Around midafternoon, we finally got enough wind to turn off the motor and start to sail, but were hard on the wind in lumpy seas and didn't get above 7 – 8 knots boat speed. This was disappointing, as the boat was capable of speeds in the low 20s.

By early evening, the wind continued to build as we approached Point Mugu/Oxnard. Our dinner of fresh fish tacos ended up being a mess, as we tried to eat and brace ourselves in the wildly pitching boat at the same time. We put the reef in shortly after dark, and turned the motor back on. We were going directly into the wind, now steady in the mid-teens, and encountering increasingly larger seas. We were now heading almost due west, along the Santa Barbara coast.

We intended to hug the shore to reduce the seaway, but that proved to be difficult. I came on again at 4:00 a.m., with the winds in the low 20s and seas 6' to 10' and very irregular. I expected ocean seas to be more regular and spaced out, but these waves were quite steep and not from a consistent direction. The boat would point to the sky at a crazy angle, then plunge down the back side, sometimes slamming hard into the next wave, then back up the next. It was like being on a roller coaster. While the boat did not roll side to side, due to being a trimaran, it still went up and down! It was not what I expected at all! Fortunately, I am not prone to seasickness or it could have been a very bad night for me.

The wind was weaving all over the place; I saw wind shifts that covered 100°. We were trying to keep the main pulling, so tacked back and forth. We also tacked into shore a couple of times to try and reduce the seaway. The autopilot was getting a workout as we tried to keep moving in the right direction. We were shooting for Conception Point, which was only about 65 miles as the crow flies, but it took us 18 hours from Oxnard! That's less than 4 knots average speed.

I have to admit, I was not comfortable in the dark with the huge seas and gusty winds, even with a bright moon. The boat felt solid enough and actually liked being at an angle to the waves. The leeward ama (float hull) would dig into the top of the wave and help stabilize the boat as it came over the crest. Going directly into the waves, it would just pitch up and down. I felt badly for the guys trying to sleep below.

* * *

Just after sunrise, Greg stuck out his head and checked in. He went back to bed, but 15 minutes later, I had to call him back up. The wind had picked up another level and I was seeing mid to high 20s on the wind readout. When it hit 30, the boat stopped, and I called him up. There was also some kind of alarm going off, which he later told me was the 35-knot alarm. (He said he didn't want to tell me what it was and freak me out, LOL.) Even with reefed main and the engine going, the boat just would not move forward. I believe there was too much windage on the three hulls and the nets.

So, we put the third reef in (the first reef had been removed, so we were actually on the second reef already.) This left about half the main up. The boat settled down and we were able to get moving again. While reefing the boat, we did two complete 360° turns, as if a monster hand had grabbed the boat and spun her around. The autopilot was on, so the rudder was fixed. I am not sure what happened: perhaps the wind caught all the windage of the hulls and just took over. It was surreal, and Greg and I looked at each other with surprise. It was unnerving to feel so out of control. I went to bed at 8:00 a.m. and was bounced out of my bunk at about 10:30. I literally caught air lying in my berth! The boat was still pitching wildly up and down, and conditions had not tempered.

We reached Point Conception about 1:00 p.m. There were three huge Coast Guard moorings there, which we weren't allowed to use. The area is odd in that it is almost completely open to the south, but protected by a little hook of land to the west and the coastline to the north. So, if the wind was blowing from the west or north, you were safe; with wind from the east or south, the anchorage would be a nightmare.

We had to anchor with a broken windlass, so Gabe and Greg had to hand-feed the 45-pound anchor, plus 50' of chain plus rode. There was no way I could have lifted the anchor, with my gut as it was. Our first attempt failed and the anchor did not set. With the wind pushing us backwards, we were easily making 3 knots the wrong way!

We tried again in shallower water. I was driving the boat, while Gabe and Greg manhandled the anchor. The second attempt worked, but we were all nervous about dragging. The wind was still solidly in the mid-20's, although the sea state was surprisingly calm in the anchorage. We watched the chartplotter and took bearings for a while to give us confidence the anchor was going to hold.

We had broken a jackstay block off the mast while putting in the last reef, so Gabe volunteered to go up the mast. The wind was still howling. We did have a power winch, so up he went. Having three hulls meant the boat didn't rock very much, but even a little at deck level means a lot when you're 30 feet off the deck. It actually turned out fine; his firefighter skills came in handy, as he kept a death grip on the mast while he was working. I thought he was crazy.

* * *

We planned to leave very early the next morning to continue up the west coast, as the wind was supposed to calm down. This would have put us in the Pacific Ocean, completely exposed to the weather. Before we left, Gabe decided to inspect the steering system, which was mostly under our aft bunk. He found a piece of the steering gear wire had frayed and was about 25% gone. There was also evidence that the pulley it was turning around had been damaged. So, Greg made the tough decision not to go around the point and up the California coast.

While the dead of night was supposed to be quiet, the wind would come back strong later in the day, with the high likelihood of big seas as well along that unprotected stretch of coast. It was too much to risk, so we decided to head back to Santa Barbara the next morning. We had seasoned burgers on cheddar jalapeño rolls with avocado. It was probably one of the top three burgers I've ever had! I got KP duty. We had a solid night's sleep, although Greg was up a couple of times to make sure we weren't dragging.

We woke up the next day facing 180° in the opposite direction, with almost no wind. We were lucky the wind hadn't picked up from the other direction; if it had, our anchor might have pulled up in the middle of the night and we would have ended up on the shore. We got underway right away and headed back to Santa Barbara, about 30 miles east. The wind stayed light the whole way, with calmer seas.

I decided to hand steer, as I thought it would be gentler on the steering gear. The autopilot wants to correct every little directional change; with hand-steering, you can let the boat find its way with less input. And being a mechanical device, the autopilot also tends to be a bit jerky. I could hand-steer and be very quiet with inputs, so as not to jolt the frayed wire. Losing steering completely would have been a real problem. The boat had an emergency tiller, but it could only be used from INSIDE the aft cabin, with no view of the outside except astern. Not very useful when docking! I frankly loved driving the boat and hogged the helm almost the whole way to Santa Barbara. Greg was going to have a professional repair company fix the steering gear, so he could continue on his way the next week.

The trip along the coast was very pretty. We were visited by schools of dolphins and seals, accompanied by a lot of birds. They were clearly chasing fish, and the birds were cleaning up their scraps. We also saw the occasional seal loafing around on the surface of the water. They would lay on their backs, eyeing us with suspicion or amusement, I am not sure which. We made it into Santa Barbara's main marina by 1:30 p.m., got diesel, and found our berth for the night. The marina was packed with mostly very nice yachts almost all over 40' (in some cases, WELL over). When I was growing up, there were few boats over 40'; now, they were a dime a dozen.

A shower on shore felt great, followed by a couple of beers and a good fish dinner. Greg and Gabe went in search of a bar, while I went to bed. I had an Amtrak train to catch at 8:00 a.m. to get to Burbank Airport for the flight home. I got up early and took a quick look at a huge monohull called Taxi Dancer. It was a famous "sled" renowned all along the west coast, with many racing victories to its credit. It was basically a glorified dinghy, 70' long with a flush deck, massive mast, and equipment. She was quite a sight.

The train was packed with kids from the University of Santa Barbara on Spring Break. The first 30 minutes were beautiful, running right along the water. Then the track turns inland and the trip was not quite so pretty. Burbank Airport was one of the worst airports I have ever been in. There wasn't nearly enough room at each gate, and the place was absolutely packed. The security arrangement was clearly a bad afterthought and was just terrible. It was a long day's travel back to Denver.

* * *

It was an amazing experience and I am glad I did it. It was definitely a bucket list kind of adventure for me. My only regret is that I wish I had been in better physical condition for such an experience. The night with wind and seas was definitely more than I had experienced before. Being dark adds tension and stress to everything, and we had an almost full moon! While I never felt like we were in any danger, I was anxious that nothing would break on my watch, which might have ended up in disaster. Caliente was a thoroughbred trimaran, but in need of a lot of work. It's definitely not what I would consider a cruising boat as the berths were barely adequate, and head and galley rudimentary. It would definitely be a blast to race with some good crew, though!

I have kept in touch with Greg, and followed his progress rebuilding a thoroughbred Farrier design called an F25C (the C meaning carbon). These boats are super light, intended as race boats, with powerful rigs. He found a very neglected boat and took on the massive job of bringing her back to life, substantially rebuilding and designing large parts of it. He made a number of excellent videos of his work, and it turned out to be absolutely incredible. I am not sure there is a finer example of the boat, and I suspect it will absolutely kill on the racecourse.

I have not heard much news about Caliente. Greg sent me a video of her in San Francisco Bay with spinnaker up, flying past another trimaran.

He had a rudimentary garden, where he grew tomatoes and some other veggies.

In the winter, he lived on a 30' cruising sloop from the '70s, which must have felt pretty plush compared to his summer lodgings, having running water and a proper head. This boat was primarily kept in the Fort Myers area, which took the brunt of Hurricane Ian in October of '22. Fred's boat ended up being washed on shore by the huge storm surge that accompanied Ian. He sent me one of the most extraordinary pictures I had ever seen in my life of his 10,000-pound boat carefully perched on its keel, high and dry, leaning against a huge tree outside a small condo building. While some of the stanchions had been crushed, there were surface scratches on the sides, and it had filled with water, causing damage to the engine, it was largely intact. Many of his friends with houses and condos had been completely wiped out, so he was actually pretty lucky in some ways.

He got most of his business from word of mouth and some craigslist ads. He would buy beat-up old boats and refurbish them; one or two were given to him by people who couldn't deal with their old boats anymore. He also did a fair amount of repair work by the hour. We kept in touch over the winter, and I suggested I could work for him part-time as an hourly employee. I was mostly familiar with the kind of work he did – fiberglass repair, boat paint, wood refurbishment, sanding, etc. After some back and forth, we agreed on $25/hour and 15 to 20 hours a week.

* * *

When he showed up in early May, I went down to his shop, and we discussed my starting in a couple of weeks. This was shortly after the Caliente delivery and my surgeries, and I was feeling pretty low energy and not a little depressed. I hoped the work would be good for me. We agreed I would work off my balance of $1,500 $25/hour at a time. This took about six weeks, as I was working closer to four hours a day three days a week, for a total of 12 hours a week. Of course, he had no shed we could work in, nor any shade, unless we rigged something up. It got into the 90s in the afternoons, and the sun beating down quickly sapped my energy. So, I worked mostly in the mornings, when it was cooler.

Fred and I got to know each other quite well. While the work was frequently noisy, using sanders and other power tools, we broke for lunch every day for 30 minutes and would chat about our lives and families, sailing and cruising. He'd had an interesting life, but lost most of his money and home in a divorce, leaving him living off what he made doing boat repair and renovation during the summers. He had adult kids who were either not interested or unwilling to help him out. It's hard to know what happens in families. He always paid me in cash, which I appreciated. The $25 an hour was actually worth more like $30 or $35 since no taxes were taken out. I ended up making about $5,000 in actual income over the summer, plus the $1,500 or so for the boat-painting work.

And the work was fun, when it wasn't too hot. I did lots of taping before painting, fiberglass, and wood sanding, and in time quite a bit of painting as well. One of our first refurb jobs was a Catalina 22 he'd bought for about $2,500. We put new bottom paint on it, painted the deck and cockpit, and I wet sanded and polished the topsides. The old gelcoat was in decent enough shape and just needed the oxidation sanded off. We removed all the wood, carefully sanded it down, and put a couple of coats of Cetol (wood oil) on it. This was a lot faster and easier than varnish, which also requires a lot of ongoing maintenance. She looked great when we were done, and he quickly found a new owner who paid him $6,500 for it. He ended up buying the boat back two years later and as of winter 2025, was still sitting in his yard.

The proximity to two train tracks meant a steady stream of noise and whistles that made me jump out of my skin. This was not a trivial thing, as he was about 400 yards from a major road crossing. The trains would blow their whistles as they approached – right next to his little yard. It was deafening and scared the crap out of me more than once. It took me weeks to become attuned to hearing the train engines coming, and to cover my ears before the whistle blew. I am pretty sure Fred was mostly deaf due to this constant barrage of noise. I can't imagine living with the noise day and night; trains go back and forth from Wyoming to the south about every 15 minutes or so, all day, every day.

I expected he would have a shop full of premium, professional quality tools. Um, no. He was a proponent of buying the cheapest crap from Harbor Freight and paying for the extended warranty. Then, when the tool inevitably died, he would get a new one for free. This was a cheap logic that appealed to the scrounger in me. It was a strategy that he used with most of his other tools, which meant that a lot of his tools were not really suitable for the tasks for which they were intended.

One of our biggest problems was the lack of water. I mostly used the rainwater for washing the boats, which had to be carted in five-gallon buckets from the back of his shack to the boats in front. Rainwater wasn't very clean to start with and we couldn't really rinse properly, so it was impossible to truly get any surface properly clean. It also meant there wasn't a real bathroom and I was having tummy problems at the time, due to the surgeries. So, that created some really anxious moments.

* * *

We took in an interesting boat called a Highlander, a 20' dinghy designed in 1949. It was a very large centerboard boat with a fiberglass hull, but finished out in wood in the interior and deck. There was no cabin, just a little covered space at the forward end of the cockpit with two huge benches on either side. It had a large main and small jib, and was raced with a spinnaker. This particular boat had been altered with some storage bins and painted many times over the years. A fiberglass over plywood floor had been installed over the fiberglass hull. While removing the benches, I realized the floor was oozing gross looking water through cracks in the fiberglass covering it.

As we explored further, we discovered that the wood underneath was completely rotted and black from being saturated with water for who knows how long. It was a nasty surprise, but not the worst we found. Insects had gotten into the wood at the base of the storage bins and laid eggs there. Ugh. We more or less had to cut out the entire interior of the boat and start over.

Fred came up with a plan to build a new floor and benches with 1 X 3 strips of wood (teak, I believe) that would allow for water to completely pass through to the bottom of the boat, where it could be easily collected and removed. He fiberglassed a series of ribs on the inside of the bottom of the hull to hold the floor up. The room under the benches could be used for storage. The whole grid structure was stained and any part that would be stood upon also had a coating of fine sand mixed in with the stain to provide a good non-slip surface.

This was actually a source of one my worst mistakes the whole summer. Fred had asked me to apply the non-skid. The process was to put down one coat of stain, sprinkle the sand on it, then put another coat over the top, bonding the sand to the wood. My mistake was not being careful enough when applying the sand, and it came out clumpy and uneven. So, I had to completely sand everything down to bare wood and start over. The second time around, we found a sugar shaker to sprinkle the sand and it came out much more evenly.

There was a beautiful rub rail all around the cockpit which we taped, sanded, and stained. The other huge job was the deck, which had a number of layers of paint applied over the years. It came off fairly easily, revealing a wooden deck in very poor condition. It had also been allowed to sit with water under the paint, and was badly cracked and discolored from years of water damage. Fred bought a sealer that he was convinced would fill in all the cracks. It was a thin sealer intended to be used as a primer, and I was convinced it was not going to provide a reasonable surface upon which to paint. I was right.

After we used his sealer and found it did very little, we applied several layers of two-part fairing compound. This came in two huge tubs that were mixed together and applied like a thick paste. Once dried, it could be sanded. The deck surface was so damaged, it took layer after layer of this material, and SO much sanding. When we finally had a reasonable surface, we applied a real primer, then three coats of white paint. It looked pretty good once we were done.

However, the next spring, we had another nasty surprise. Cracks had appeared through the multiple layers of fairing compound, primer, and paint. The deck had obviously needed to sit and completely dry out in a protected area for months, maybe a year, before we did the work. We were crushed.

Fortunately, the owner was very understanding and stopped in a number of times to see the progress, which he was very pleased with. Plus, he was paying time and materials, and Fred was being very kind about how much time we'd spent on this classic old boat. The whole thing had to be sanded, and the cracks filled with thickened epoxy and re-painted. It did look good when we were done. I don't know if any more cracks showed up after that, as Fred and I parted ways shortly after the re-paint. Which is another story….

* * *

We finished the first year on good terms, and I agreed to come back the next year, which was 2023. His usual start date was early May. I had a number of major events coming up that May, including a high school graduation, a college graduation in New York City, and my daughter graduating from nursing school (which also included a celebratory dinner with the whole family.) The high school graduation involved Kathy's daughter and boyfriend coming to Denver for 10 days. It was a very busy time for me, and I let Fred know months ahead that I would only be able to work a couple days a week that month, and would obviously be out of town for a week in May as well.

Once he returned to Colorado, we got back to work. However, he began pressing me for more hours. While I did what I could, my primary focus was on my family and the celebrations that month.

The graduation dinner for my daughter was on May 27th, a Saturday. I received a voicemail during the dinner from Fred saying that I needed to come get my stuff on Monday, which was to be my last day. I had loaned him my compressor as his had died, and there were a few other of my personal items that I used daily. The next week was Memorial Day and I had to take our visitors to the airport, so had only scheduled two days with him.

I emailed him when I got home and suggested I come over Sunday, which is what I did. He simply said that he needed more hours, and that apparently was that, as far as he was concerned. I asked him if he had someone else lined up, since I assumed he would have had said something to me if he did. He said vaguely that he had some "potential leads out there" and nothing else.

To be honest, I was completely gob-smacked, as the Brits say. There had been no warning of his state of mind, and we certainly hadn't had any real conversation about him needing more hours or he would have to find someone else. It made no sense to me for him to get rid of me, even if he DID have someone else interested in working for him. It was an odd work situation in any case. He needed to find someone who knew something about the work, and would be OK working part-time and in such a rudimentary location. I considered Fred to be a friend, and for him to end it like he did really upset me.

As it turned out, as with so many things, it was for the best. Kathy and I were looking at selling our home and finding a new one, and decided to remodel our kitchen. I ended up more or less managing the project for the whole month of August, which would have precluded my working with him during that period of time. I did try to email Fred the next year just to touch base, and was hoping to open up a line of communication. I felt like things were left very much unresolved, at least from my point of view. He never responded. I was tempted to show up at his lot and see if he would talk, which I did in summer, 2025. The whole event had not impacted him as it had me, and he didn't remember much of the details. We had a nice chat and I felt better about how it all turned out.

Part of what may have fed into this was that the paint job he'd done on my own boat went to complete crap after one season. I'd shown him pictures of the work and shared my distress at how poorly it had held up. Before he painted, I had sanded the topsides, the area between the water line and the toe rail. This had been painted blue and held up pretty well even though, as it turned out, he had not used a primer. I took great care in sanding the old paint to make sure the surface would accept new paint readily. He did not do this prep work on the deck and cockpit, and all the areas that were non-skid quickly started peeling, exposing the yellow underneath.

By the end of the first season, much of the white had peeled up and was a terrible mess and has continued to get worse since. It was obvious to me that he had neither sanded the non-skid areas properly nor primed anything. Boat paint is not like most paints used around the house. They have to stand up to very harsh conditions, and are designed to layer up with a primer and top coat of paint. When I bought the paint, he was very excited that I'd bought good paint from Pettit. He mostly used cheap Rustoleum, which to my mind was not appropriate for boating applications. Obviously, I also needed to buy primer and define better that the work needed to be done properly. Now, I am going to have to re-do all of the white-painted areas (which as of this writing, hasn't yet been done).

Chapter Fifteen
My Boat Almost Sinks

Following the disappointing end with Fred, it turned out another of his decisions led to one of the worst events in my boating life. My boat was at Pelican Bay Marina and had been largely ignored all summer. I just didn't have the time. And with the paint peeling up, it just didn't feel like a place where I wanted to spend time.

I got a call from the marina manager that he thought the boat was taking on water, and his worker had pumped out a bunch already. I went down to the marina to find the boat down by a foot at the stern. This is not a big boat, so I think is fair to say it was sinking. Being a trimaran, the two float hulls had kept her from going under, and were buoyant enough that I could get on board.

At first, I didn't understand what had happened. The boat did not have a bilge pump, and there were watertight areas fore and aft. But the area under the cockpit was open, so if water got high enough, it could also fill the cockpit, which is what happened. There was a LOT of water on board for such a small boat – I estimated several hundred gallons. I had two batteries I used for a trolling motor to get the boat on and off the dock, but they were in a storage area forward of the cockpit, completely submerged.

Being a big Ryobi fan, I'd bought a transfer pump, which is a battery-powered water pump intended to be used anywhere you need to move water around. I used it as a portable bilge pump when water got in the boat, or somehow into the amas or float hulls. It used a simple ¾" garden hose-type fitting, and while not particularly fast, it could run for well over an hour on one battery. I'd brought this with me and started it up. It turned out to be a lifesaver, as it emptied the boat over the course of the next two hours. I also used a manual pump on the stern locker.

One of the problems I uncovered was that one of the cockpit drain plugs had cracked and was letting water in. It was always a conflict for me as to whether or not to leave the plugs in. They were very close to the water line and when the lake got wavy at the dock, water would come in. On the other hand, if it rained, the cockpit could fill up.

Once enough water was out of the boat so that it was sitting more or less on its lines again, water stopped coming in the cockpit drains. I still hadn't figured out what happened, but I needed to get it out of the water ASAP; I was pretty sure whatever had caused the problem was not fixed; I was concerned there was a hole somewhere else that was letting water in.

I called Kathy to bring the truck down. Since the boat batteries were dead, we couldn't use the electric motor to get over to the ramp. Fortunately, at only 1,400 pounds, the boat was not hard to paddle. So, with Luka along, we quickly covered the half mile or so. We had launched and retrieved the boat several times by now and had a pretty good process down. The amas needed to be folded at the dock, which involved removing four 8"x½" bolts, two for each support beam. It's an ingenious system designed by Ian Farrier in the '70s. My boat was one of the earliest to use the system and it worked smoothly every time.

I was worried that the drain plug had somehow come out, but that was not the case. We got the boat on the trailer and up the ramp. Then, we pulled the drain plug at the base of the skeg – basically the very bottom of the boat. Water drained out for the next 45 minutes, even after having pumped for several hours.

We towed the boat back to the house and left it in the street for the night. The next day, I came out to inspect it more carefully. I discovered that the two bolts that held the base of the rudder to the boat via a bracket were completely rusted through. The bottom bracket was at the water line, so was submerged much of the time.

Fred and I had installed these new in the spring, and it had been a real pain in the butt. The bottom bracket was at the very back and bottom of the stern locker. The hatch for this locker was on the starboard side, about 3" from the bracket location. The locker was too small to completely crawl into, so you had to lay on your back, with your legs sticking out of the hatch. You then had to hold the nut over your head, while someone else turned the bolt on the outside. Fred, to his credit, was much thinner than me by about 25 pounds and he had volunteered to get in the locker. That gave me the easy job. In hindsight, I wish we had thought this through more carefully.

In the five months or so that the boat had been sitting in the water, the bolts had completely corroded through, allowing water into the stern locker. This pulled the boat down far enough to allow water in the cockpit drain – the same one with the cracked drain plug. Once the cockpit overfilled into the space below the cockpit floor, the boat must have filled to the brim, saved only by the float hulls.

The bolts were stainless steel, but the two little spacers the bracket sat on were aluminum. In the presence of water, this would create corrosion. It was stunning that they had corroded to roughly half their normal width in such a short time; I had to use a cutting blade to cut off the heads. To be fair, this was something I should have thought about. I had not touched the original bolts since purchase about four years earlier, so it's hard to know what had been used prior that. Whatever it was, obviously it lasted much longer. Maybe there had been a plastic or rubber washer in place that helped. I also think using something besides aluminum for the spacers would have solved the problem.

Amazingly, one of the batteries seemed to still be holding a charge, while the other appeared to be completely dead. At over $100 for each battery, this was a bummer. But in retrospect, I was really lucky this whole event didn't turn out worse. I had visions of the boat sinking at the dock, in the dirty brown water of Cherry Creek Reservoir. It wasn't deep at the dock, perhaps 8', but you could not see past the end of your arm in the disgusting water. It would have been very difficult to get the boat back up and floating with my own resources. I was very thankful to the marina staff for giving me the heads up, and for getting a good start on the pumping – which they did with a manual pump.

* * *

It was not the first time one of my boats had sunk. OK, to be fair, this one did not sink, but it was close. When my son Marc was about 8 years old, I wanted to get him involved in sailing, like my dad had me. I didn't have a boat, so was sailing on other guys' boats – ChuckWagon, Blue Side Down, etc. These were activities I did without my family. My ex was not interested in sailing, so it was up to Marc to carry on the family tradition.

I bought a Day Sailer locally that needed quite a bit of work. There was damage at the aft of the centerboard case, and generally she was pretty rough. The Day Sailer is a large dinghy with a small cuddy/storage area at the forward end of the cockpit, which is huge. They have been built since 1956 and are still being built, with over 10,000 being sold. While she was only 575 pounds, she was very beamy. By all reports, she had a lot of form stability, which meant the shape of her hull would make her hard to tip over.

It was the first time I had really done any fiberglass work, and it was a lot of fun. After much sanding, and applying epoxy and fiberglass, I had satisfactorily repaired the centerboard case. She also needed some new bottom paint, so I asked three buddies to come over. We flipped her upside down, and I applied spanking new white paint to her bottom.

Owning that boat did not have the desired effect, as Marc never really caught the bug as I had done. Perhaps one event really helped to discourage him. We had taken the boat out for some practice. Being so light, she was easy to rig and launch. The mast could be manhandled into place, unlike most of the keelboats I had owned or sailed on that required some sort of raising system.

We were on Cherry Creek Reservoir, the handiest piece of water in Denver. Winds were brisk, in the 10 – 12 knots range, and we were having a good time blasting around. When the time came to go in, winds were starting to gust to the high teens, and we headed down wind to go home. Under main and jib only, we were planing along on port, which was exhilarating. I was sitting well back, knowing I needed to keep the bow from burying. All of a sudden, we were both in the water and the boat was on her side.

I still have not figured out what happened. We capsized to port or in the direction we were hiking out. We had not gybed by accident, or been pulled over to starboard by a huge gust. The only thing I can think of is that the wind shifted forward and I didn't bear away. So, as it went forward, my weight started to pull the boat over. Then, I pulled on the tiller as I fell back, and she came over on top of us. We had our PFDs on, of course, but it was a real shock to go from having a lot fun to being in the lake.

The boat quickly went from on her side to completely turtle, with her mast facing down and the centerboard sticking up in the air. Problem was, the mast was longer than the depth of the lake at that point, so it stuck hard in the mud. No amount of pulling and pushing (and swearing) would bring her back upright. With the sails also resisting my efforts, she was not going anywhere.

Fortunately, a kindly couple on a power boat came over to offer assistance. I rigged up a line to the beam of the boat and they backed down, pulling her upright. The mast came up with several pounds of disgusting mud stuck to her tip. They also were kind enough to tow us back to the ramp, after we bailed most of the water out. While no one was harmed, we were both very cold and a bit shocked. I prided myself on being a good sailor and in control of most situations, so this one threw me for a loop. What enthusiasm Marc had was replaced with doubt. I sold the boat shortly thereafter at a nice profit, given the work I had put into her. Unlike many of the boats I'd owned or had been in the family, I was not sorry to see this one go. It had not been a great choice in the first place, but I did enjoy working on her.

Chapter Sixteen
The Far East 26

We lived on the southeast side of Denver for many years. All the kids from our blended family had gone to the excellent Cherry Creek schools and the last one, Luka, was to graduate in 2023. Kathy and I started thinking about moving. We were close to Centennial Airport, with a number of flight schools that ran single-engine Cessna trainers over our home all day most days. There had been a midair crash to the north of us in 2022, so they changed their flight paths to concentrate over our neighborhood and those close to us. It was insufferable.

On nice weather days (which was most days), over 500 flights a day flew over our home, usually at 500 feet altitude. I worked at home, so this was terrible. No amount of complaining made any difference. So, this was a primary reason that I wanted to move.

We also had some sketchy neighbors who kept 12 to 14 vehicles on the street, even though the homes only had two-car garages. Many of these vehicles were in disrepair. Plus, our house was very close to our neighbors on all sides. Our 1980s home was built on a very small lot and while we mostly liked the home itself, all the above factors led us to want to move.

* * *

Carter Lake is north of Denver about 30 miles, just west of Loveland. Unlike Cherry Creek Reservoir, where the water is pretty nasty, Carter Lake's water is from snow runoff, so is clear and clean. I'd never sailed on Carter in all the years I'd lived in Colorado, so I was determined to do so. Carter is roughly 2 ½ miles by about ¾ of a mile and has a nice marina and a sailing club, called appropriately enough Carter Lake Sailing Club. They have an active racing group, so I contacted the Commodore, who put me in touch with Bridger, one of the newer members of the Sailing Club. Bridger had a cool racing boat (More on that later) and was in need of crew, so I volunteered to come along the next time they went out.

We started looking for our new home a full year before we were ready to move. We wanted to get a sense of what properties were available and at what price. We really wanted at least half an acre with nice views. We weren't too fussy about being in the mountains or the plains, but wanted to be close to Carter Lake. What we found was very disappointing. So many homes were in need of major remodeling, especially the kitchens and bathrooms. At the price point we were considering, we didn't think we should have to also spend $100,000 (or more!) in remodeling. While many were on more than an acre, the neighbors frequently felt close because of the way the homes were positioned on their lots.

We saw a few places that were disgusting, even at close to (or over) a $1 million asking price. We visited a home on 20 acres just outside of Lyons. The property was spectacular and the Zillow pictures looked pretty good, with the biggest drawback being the home was pretty small. There was a huge horse barn that was actually larger than the home! The asking price was $1.2 million. When we visited it in person, we realized that the pictures had clearly been taken in the past, as what we saw almost didn't look like the same place. The barn was nicer than the house by a lot, even though it had clearly been neglected as well.

Kathy went into the house before the Realtor and I did, and came out a few minutes later with a disgusted look on her face. We were greeted in the entrance area by leaking skylights that had destroyed the drywall and damaged the floor. The basement had a mouse/rat infestation; the drywall and wall insulation had been torn out of the walls in several places and was spread out across the basement floor. There were mouse droppings everywhere, and it smelled. There was lots of evidence of water intrusion, and the mechanical space was a mess. We were stunned. The property had been on the market for over a year, and even though we could see past the grossness, the asking price just didn't make sense. So, we passed. We learned later it sold for $900,000. I felt sorry for the new buyers.

While that was the worst example, we found many others that were in a similar condition. The few that were "move in ready" were either out of our price range or still needed major work. We expanded our search to include the foothills west of Denver and to the south, toward Colorado Springs.

A property came up in Palmer Lake, a little town west of Monument and about 15 miles north of Colorado Springs. From here, Kathy would have about a 40-minute commute to her job. If we had moved north, she would probably have had to find a new job. The new home was on 2 ½ acres and snuggled quite close to the foothills, in the shadow of Mount Herman. We quickly made a successful offer and moved in mid-2024.

The only problem was, there was no place to sail. Palmer Lake has a tiny lake of about 30 acres that was jammed with SUPs during the summer and not suitable for any kind of sailboat. Pueblo is a nice reservoir of about 5,000 acres, but was over an hour to the south. So, my sailing activities would have to be put on hold for a while.

* * *

Bridger was a graduate of Cherry Creek High School (Same as my kids) and lived in the Fort Collins area, which is about 20 miles north of Loveland. He owned one of the most unique and rare boats in the U.S., a Far East 26'. It had been built in China and was considered a sport boat. Roughly comparable to the J-80, it had a very nice cabin, with decent berths for four and an enclosed head. Oddly, there was no galley and it was quite a bit heavier than a J-80, at 3,650 pounds versus 2,900 pounds. But with a decent cruising cabin space, it was an appealing design.

Boats built in China have a general reputation for being of poor quality, but the Far East was the exception. Not only was the quality of the glass work exceptional throughout, it had some of the best hardware: Harken hardware and a Selden mast. The interior woodwork was of a very high quality. The nonskid was excellent. And it came from the factory with North sails.

Bridger replaced the original sails with excellent North 3Di sails, which not only looked amazing in their all-black color, but performed like no Dacron or Mylar sails I'd ever used. There was almost zero stretch and they kept their shape extremely well. The boats were selling for around $50,000 new in 2014, which at the time was an absolute steal. To Bridger's knowledge, there were only three in the United States, and two of them were on little Carter Lake! Unfortunately, the other boat did not race.

The boat had a relatively small furling jib, a large square-topped main, and had been converted to an asymmetrical spinnaker from the factory symmetrical. This was for ease of use, but I am not sure it worked out as planned. The asym was an absolute beast at almost 600 square feet, and was very difficult to trim in anything over 15 knots. The point of a sport boat is to be able to plane off wind, but we were never able to do it. Maybe it was just too heavy.

One curiosity of the boat was that it had a lifting keel. But unlike most lifting keels, this could only be done at the dock, with a weird aluminum-framed contraption that had to be set up before and after every sail. The keel could not be raised or lowered in the water, and it was quite a process to set up the winch frame and crank up the keel, which weighed over 1,300 pounds, and so took a lot of effort.

Another oddity was that the square-topped main did not clear the backstay. During every tack, the backstay had to be let off so the main would pass through, then pulled back on once we were on the new tack. It was a real handful for the person on the helm who had to pull the traveler up, steer the boat, and also mess with the backstay. When it was blowing, it was not really something one person could do.

We raced a few regattas and like so many racing sailboats, Bridger's crew was interesting and fun to hang out with. Bridger was a very successful financial planner. The guy he preferred to let helm was John, a mid-40s guy who had already retired as a result of great planning, smart investing, and having no children! Mick was an Aussie and true to the reputation, was a real character and serial entrepreneur. It was a lot of fun being around guys with such diverse backgrounds.

The problem was, the boat was lumped in with other sport boats, but being so heavy, it didn't perform like one. (Or maybe we didn't know how to sail it like a sport boat.) We were competitive upwind and in light airs, but going downwind, we generally gave up quite a bit to the competition. With a PHRF rating of 120, we were rated with the J-80, which was much lighter and more established. Of course, there was no rigging guide, so we had to guess about rig tension and setup. The J-80 has small books written about those subjects.

On our little Carter Lake, we usually did pretty well, frequently finishing first overall. But we'd lose on handicap because we had to beat the other boats by so much. Still, any day sailing beats any day working, and spending the time with Bridger, John, and Mick was never boring.

Chapter Seventeen

America's Cup, SailGP and Rolex, Vendée Globe, and the Ultimes

AMERICA'S CUP

I first started watching the America's Cup in 1983, when Alan Bond took the Cup away from the New York Yacht Club, after they had held the trophy for 132 years. This was the first year they were able to broadcast the event live, or close to it. Twelve-meter yachts had been used since 1958, and the class was well-established as the America's Cup boat of choice. Of course, this favored the defender, as they were able to make the rules. The next challenge was four years later in Perth, Australia in 1987, when Dennis Conner, representing the San Diego Yacht Club, clobbered the Aussies 4-0. The Cup would never be the same.

ESPN had live coverage from Perth in the middle of the night, and my VCR was working overtime. I even stayed up into the wee hours to watch the final races. This was also the first time they had cameras on board, although nothing like we have today. Perth was a great venue, with lots of wind and big waves. It was exciting sailboat racing, and good TV.

The next race was the silly giant (137') monohull of KZ-1 against Dennis Conner's less-giant catamaran. Conner easily won 2-0. Credit to SDYC that after that they decided to change the boats to a much larger and faster International America's Cup Class (IACC), which were to be the boats used for the next 15 years. These large monohulls (82') were fast, but it was clear that for the Cup to get through to a wider audience, they needed something faster and more dangerous. The AC 72 was born, the first foiling catamaran used in the Cup, and it was a revelation. Top speeds went from 12 to 15 knots to 30 to 40. The finals were held close to the shore in San Francisco Bay, where thousands of spectators were able to watch, and it was a true spectacle. Oracle Team USA came back from 8-0 down to win the Cup in 2013 9-8, which surely ranks as one of the greatest comebacks in sporting history.

The TV graphics and telemetry off the boats were also improved, to help non-sailors follow along. You didn't have to be a sailboat racer to understand what was happening on the water. At the same time, GoPro-like cameras allowed TV coverage to greatly expand and go onboard from many different angles. It brought what can be a difficult sport to understand into people's living rooms. It also demonstrated the incredible speeds and dynamic nature of these amazing boats.

The 72s were amazing, but there was an effort to make racing more accessible to more countries and teams. So, they shrank the concept to 50' and reduced the onboard crews from 11 to 6. The 2017 Cup was held on the Great Sound in Bermuda, a brilliant venue, well protected but also easily accessible for spectators. There was also an America's Cup World Series, the second time AC boats were raced as a fleet. (The first was in 2013.) In my opinion, this was more interesting than the Cup match racing itself, which tended to be very one-sided. A boat with even a slight speed advantage tended to sail off into the distance, making the actual America's Cup racing pretty boring. Fleet racing increased the opportunities for boats to mix it up, and created lots of drama at mark roundings and crossings.

New Zealand won the 2017 America's Cup with a clear design and speed advantage, and took the Cup back home. Since the defender can decide which boats are to be used, they scrapped the AC50 in favor of a foiling monohull, the AC75. I thought this was a huge mistake, as the AC50 had proven to be incredibly fast and relatively cheap. Continued development of an existing class would have been a far better approach than starting over with a completely new class.

They would have attracted many more nations to participate with a proven, cheap design.

My concerns were immediately evident from the very start of the 2021 Challenger Series. Race after race turned into a parade, as any minor speed advantage was amplified at speeds that were regularly over 40 knots. Classic match racing was barely seen and the racing was very boring, even for an America's Cup nerd like me. New Zealand easily won again.

They threw a wrench in the works when they announced the next Cup would be held in Barcelona. While the people of New Zealand howled in protest, the New Zealand team recognized that an America's Cup held on the far side of the world in a tiny country with limited resources was not good for the expansion of the Cup. Barcelona is one of Europe's biggest sailing cities, and the decision turned out to be a good one. Many thousands of people flocked to the city to see the racing, which was now expanded to include a new class, the AC40, as well as Women's and Youth regattas, which were immensely entertaining. The AC75 was now pretty well developed, and the huge, crazy-looking foils on each side added a dramatic flair to the boats. The AC40 was a four-person boat, but along the same design lines as its bigger sister and almost as fast.

The Youth and Women's events were comprised of 12 teams: six America's Cup teams that aligned with the big AC teams and what they called Invited teams. There was quite a disparity from the top to the bottom, with some teams not getting very much practice time in the boats. But the fleet racing was, once again, incredibly competitive and full of drama. The two groups were narrowed down to six semi-final races, then a match race to decide the champion. Italy won both the Youth Cup, with American Magic just behind, and the women's event, with Great Britain finishing second. This was a great step forward for the America's Cup program, as the predominantly male (and older) sailors dominated racing at the highest level has needed a boost of new blood for a long time. Now, if they could figure out how to include people of color...

Boats were now going upwind at 30 to 40 knots and downwind close to (and over) 50 knots. Closing speeds when tacking were 80 knots+ in some cases, which led to a new level of risk and expertise from the world's best sailors. The racing this time was a lot closer, with the Challenger series going right down to the wire. The actual final proved that the Kiwis still had an edge over the rest of the world and they beat INEOS Brittania 7-2. New Zealand has the choice of where to hold the next Cup.

SAILGP

Larry Ellison, a longtime fan of top sailing (and the America's Cup), and Russell Coutts, a successful America's Cup competitor and world-class sailor, saw the brilliance of the AC50 and started a new Grand Prix league, SailGP. They limited the boats to a one-design boat designed, maintained, and operated by the SailGP organization. This ensured races were won and lost by sailors, not designers. Also, all technical information, including on-the-water data, is shared by all teams. Unlike the paranoid, secretive world of the America's Cup, this was a breath of fresh air. Season 1 started with six teams and grew to 12 in 2025. Venues are all over the world and tend to favor places where the racing can be brought close to shore so that spectators can attend.

The boats are heavily sponsored and TV coverage is excellent, with quality on-the-water video and commentary. There are five to seven fleet races over two days, giving every team a chance to make the three-team final. Races are kept short, about 15 minutes, so they can get in three or four in an afternoon. Points are awarded at every regatta, then the best three teams over the whole series have a final sail off, winner takes all, with a $2 million prize. The fleet racing is incredibly good, with so many teams and so many world-class sailors.

The top speed ever achieved is about 55 knots. The America's Cup and Sail GP boats, have reached a practical speed limit with foils. Apparently at 50 knots+, the water literally boils (called cavitation) on the foils! I expect that some smart person will figure out a solution to this, and there will be another leap in performance. Obviously, 50 knots is nothing to sneeze at. In 2010 the fastest ANY sailboat had ever gone was about 50 knots! In 2025 the record is 65.45 knots by Vestas Sailrocket.

Another amazing stat is that they can sail at four to five times the wind speed, especially when it's light. They can start to foil in about 6.5 knots and go 30+ knots down wind. Most monohulls can only dream of that kind of performance, and even performance multihulls are lucky to do wind speed. My only gripe is that in their effort to appeal to the average sports fan, speeds are delivered in kilometers per hour, not knots. But it's a small price to pay for such amazing sailing and spectacle.

ROLEX

The watchmaker has been a sponsor and supporter of yachting for many years, and are the leading sponsor for several of the largest offshore races: Fastnet, Sidney to Hobart, Middle Sea Race, and the China Sea Race, all of which are about 600 miles and in some of the world's toughest sailing areas. They also sponsor the Rolex Swan Cup, Big Boat Series, and a number of other top international regattas and events.

The offshore events include some of the world's finest and fastest yachts, especially some monster 100' monohulls. These are privately owned by millionaires, with paid crew and the best international sailors and navigators in the world, many of whom come from the America's Cup and SailGP ranks. The starts of these races, including the Caribbean 600 and the Transpac, are broadcast and can be incredible spectacles, with hundreds of boats on the line. Of course, amateurs can also enter by meeting some safety and long-distance sailing requirements. So, while the millionaires compete for the top prizes, it's still possible for a well-prepared and sailed amateur boat to walk away with silver in a smaller class.

Sailboat racing is one of the few areas of competition where amateurs can line up next to the rich and famous, and best sailors in the world. Can you imagine a guy building a car in his garage, then lining up on a Formula 1 grid? Or a farmer bringing his horse to the Kentucky Derby?

VENDÉE GLOBE

One racing competition where amateurs and professionals do NOT line up together is the Vendée Globe. What once was a Corinthian race for allcomers, it has now evolved into a highly professional, full-time enterprise for large teams of sailors, designers, builders, and on-shore support staff. Sailed in the Imoca 60, it's a solo around-the-world race, without stops or support. The top Imoca 60s are full foiling yachts capable of top speeds in the 40s and sustained speeds in the mid 20s.

During the 2024/25 Vendée Nicolas Lunven broke the outright solo 24-hour speed record at 546.60 nautical miles, for an average speed of 22.78 knots. This is an astonishing pace, especially considering it was done by a solo sailor! These huge boats carry massive amounts of sail, with a giant mainsail and up to three genoas and jibs, as well as down wind sails. The management and skill required for these sailors to keep the boat driving under all conditions is seriously amazing. With high-speed internet available all over the planet, and tiny, high quality cameras like the GoPro, we are able to come along for the ride and get daily updates.

The current generation of the Imoca has dispensed with the traditional cockpit and brought the sailors inside, under a hard-top canopy. All lines come here, to a central bank of winches. This small area also acts as the sleeping berth, head, galley, and saloon. The Imocas have windows and incredible electronics packages, so sailors can monitor the boat and their progress from inside. Some of their daily updates are astonishing, with the decks awash above and behind them, and tons of water coming over the bow as they charge along at 20+ knots, with rooster tails disappearing astern.

These are special individuals, requiring not only keen sailing skill but marathon endurance, both physical and mental. While the original around-the-world race winner was Robin Knox-Johnston, who completed the journey in 312 days, the record before the 24/25 race was 74 days and 3 hours, done in a non-foiling boat. Charlie Dalin won the 2025 Vendée in 63 days, 9 hours, beating the old around-the-world record by over nine days. Jules Verne wrote a famous book about going Around the World in 80 Days. Now, a solo sailor has done that easily!

ULTIMES

While the Imocas are amazing boats, they are a step behind the true greyhounds of the sea – the Ultimes. These 100' monster trimarans hold all ocean-going records. François Gabart holds the solo around-the-world record in Macif at 42 days, 16 hours, and 40 minutes. Amazingly, this is only a day and half slower than the fully crewed record by Francois Joyon on IDEC 3. Ultimes have also gone full foiling and are achieving maximum speeds of over 50 knots! Like the America's Cup and SailGP foiling boats, they have found that cavitation on their foils restricts their ultimate speed potential. If you haven't seen these boats in action, a trip to YouTube is in order! Unfortunately, they struggle with reliability, as foils and rudders are damaged by junk in the oceans.

About the Author

Mike Mendes' story begins in San Tomé, Venezuela, where a childhood shaped by global moves—thanks to his father's career in the oil industry—took him from the deserts of Tripoli, Libya to the bustling heart of London, England. Along the way, one passion took hold early and never let go: sailing the warm, blue waters of the Mediterranean, a love that would chart the course of his next six decades.

Mike went on to study at the University of Denver, earning a BA in Environmental Science, and launched his career in solar and environmentally focused industries. When the solar boom of the early 1980s dimmed, he pivoted to the rapidly rising world of technology, spending 15 successful years in computer product and service sales—eventually leading and mentoring teams of other sales professionals.

But by 2000, as the tech bubble collapsed, Mike felt called toward something more hands-on and personally meaningful. That drive led him into home remodeling, where he spent years helping homeowners improve the spaces they lived in—selling windows, siding, roofing, and general contracting services.

In 2017, Mike took his boldest professional step yet: launching his own kitchen remodeling business. Partnering with a seasoned general contractor, he focused on what he does best—connecting with clients, shaping inspired designs, and guiding projects from concept to contract. The result has been a period of both creative fulfillment and lasting success.

Through every career chapter, one constant has remained: the call of the water. Mike continued to seek out sailing adventures big and small, exploring coastlines across the country on boats of all kinds and with countless companions. In 2023, he began capturing his most unforgettable journeys on paper.

Those stories became this book—an invitation to share in a lifetime of wind, water, and adventure.

www.ingramcontent.com/pod-product-compliance
Lightning Source LLC
LaVergne TN
LVHW010917110826
845149LV00013B/2394

* 9 7 8 1 9 6 6 1 9 1 3 7 7 *